Decarbonising Energy

The Pathway to Net Zero

Author
Hugo Lidbetter

Managing director
Sian O'Neill

Decarbonising Energy: The Pathway to Net Zero
is published by

Globe Law and Business Ltd
3 Mylor Close
Horsell
Woking
Surrey GU21 4DD
United Kingdom
Tel: +44 20 3745 4770
www.globelawandbusiness.com

Printed and bound in Great Britain by Ashford Colour Press Ltd

Decarbonising Energy: The Pathway to Net Zero

ISBN 9781787423589
EPUB ISBN 9781787423596
Adobe PDF ISBN 9781787423602
Mobi ISBN 9781787423619

Table of contents

I. **Introduction** 9

II. **The global energy triumvirate: greenhouse gas emissions, global warming and green energy** 13

1. **Global energy trends – overview** 13

2. **Green shoots still to bud: carbon far from dated** 14

2.1 The coal problem 14
2.2 Global greenhouse gas emissions (GHGEs) and global warming 16

3. **Global green energy: an investment success story?** 20

3.1 Investment in renewables 20
3.2 Growing capacity 21
3.3 Back to the future (again) 22
3.4 Capacity is not power 23
3.5 Electrifying energy 24

4. Renewable technology: now cheaper and more efficient 25

4.1 Falling costs 25
4.2 Explaining the cost savings 27
4.3 Price competition and the path to diminishing marginal returns 29

5. Global wrap-up 31

III. How green is UK energy? 33

1. UK energy trends – overview 33

2. Energy versus electricity 34

2.1 Generation capacity and interconnectors 35
2.2 Electricity generated 37

3. The relationship between capacity and electricity generated in the UK 40

IV. UK policy and the road to Net Zero 41

1. UK energy policy 41

2. Policy development – overview 42

2.1 Climate Change Act 2008 42
2.2 Coalition government 2011 budget 42
2.3 Electricity Market Reform (EMR) under the Energy Act 2013 42
2.4 The Renewables Obligation (RO) 44
2.5 The Feed-in Tariff (FiT) 45
2.6 Smart Export Guarantee (SEG) 45

3. The emergence of Net Zero 46

4. The Committee on Climate Change's 2019 Progress Report .. 49

5. Future energy scenarios 2019: Net Zero aspects 50

5.1 Heating homes 51
5.2 Growth in generation capacity 52
5.3 Net Zero actually means negative zero – sequestration 53
5.4 Indispensability of carbon capture, use and storage (CCUS) technology 53

5.5 Electric vehicles (EVs) 54
5.6 Interoperability 55
5.7 Behavioural 55

6. Delivering Net Zero 55

V. Generation technologies: going from black to grey 57

1. Overview 57

2. Coal-fired generation 58

2.1 Summary 58
2.2 The coal scene 58
2.3 Policy 58
2.4 Convert or close 60
2.5 Biomass conversion, gas conversion and carbon capture, use and storage (CCUS) 61
2.6 Decommissioning 61

3. Nuclear generation 63

3.1 Overview 63
3.2 New build nuclear 64
3.3 Nuclear development costs 65
3.4 Nuclear third-party liability 66
3.5 Brexit and Euratom ('Brexatom') 67
3.6 The regulated asset base (RAB) model 68
3.7 What next for RAB? 70

4. Natural gas-fired generation 70

4.1 Overview 70
4.2 Peaking plants 72
4.3 Baseload plants 72
4.4 The Capacity Market (CM): a capacity lost? 73
4.5 Gas in a renewables world? 73
4.6 Gas: going green? 75

VI. Generation technologies: going from grey to green 77

1. Overview 77

2. Solar photovoltaic (PV) 78

2.1 Overview 78
2.2 Why solar? 79

2.3 Development aspects 79
2.4 Operation aspects 80
2.5 Connection aspects and stranded assets 80
2.6 Solar and subsidy 81
2.7 Solar without subsidy 85

3. Wind power 87

3.1 Overview 87
3.2 Wind in the UK 88
3.3 Cost of wind 89
3.4 Investing in wind power 91
3.5 Wind: finance aspects 94

VII. Net Zero and future technologies 97

1. Overview 97

2. Energy storage 98

2.1 Overview 98
2.2 Opportunities: co-location and revenue stacking 98
2.3 Battery storage: lithium ion and electric vehicles (EVs) 99
2.4 Pumped storage 100
2.5 Thermal storage 101
2.6 Hydrogen storage 102

3. Floating wind power 102

3.1 Overview 102
3.2 Early stage technology 102
3.3 Crown Estate and floating projects 103
3.4 Floating wind as a sector opportunity 103
3.5 Floating wind benefits 104
3.6 Key issues with floating projects 105
3.7 What next for floating wind? 106

4. Hydrogen: to the rescue? 107

4.1 Why hydrogen? 107
4.2 How is hydrogen produced? 108
4.3 Hydrogen and energy storage 112
4.4 Applications of clean hydrogen 112
4.5 Hydrogen: two opportunities 115
4.6 Hydrogen in 2050 116

5. Carbon capture technology 118

5.1 Overview 118
5.2 Carbon capture storage (CCS) and Net Zero 119

6. Negative emissions 121

6.1 Going green: reforestation and rewilding 122
6.2 Direct air capture (DAC) 123
6.3 Bioenergy carbon capture storage (BECCS) 123

7. Advanced nuclear technologies 124

7.1 Overview 124
7.2 Small modular reactors (SMRs) (Generation III water-cooled SMRs) 125
7.3 Advanced modular reactors (AMRs) (Generation IV AMRs) 126
7.4 Why advanced nuclear? 126

VIII. The UK's electricity network: electrons in balance 129

1. Overview 129

2. The electricity system: what it is and how it works 130

2.1 Generators 130
2.2 Transmission operators (TOs) 130
2.3 Transmission system operator (TSO) 131
2.4 Distribution network operators (DNOs) 131
2.5 Trade and aggregators 131
2.6 Suppliers 132
2.7 Customers (industrial, commercial and residential) 132
2.8 Ofgem and the Department for Business, Energy and Industrial Strategy (BEIS) 133

3. Balancing the electricity system: the balancing mechanism (BM) and ancillary services 133

3.1 The balancing mechanism (BM) 133
3.2 Wind and the balancing mechanism (BM) 135
3.3 Ancillary services 136

IX. Looking forward 145

Notes 148
About the author 151
About Globe Law and Business 152

Acknowledgements

A number of people have been very generous with their time in the preparation of this Special Report. Many offered to review sections of the report and have provided very helpful perspectives and comments on a number of the issues. As mentioned in the report, there is no silver bullet when it comes to achieving Net Zero, and there is accordingly a spectrum of opinion on what it will take to decarbonise our electricity system and electrify more of our energy supply. This includes deciding what an optimal power mix should look like, how much of final energy demand should be accounted for by electricity (as opposed to, say, decarbonised gas), what it means for smarter networks and how much emphasis should be given to delivering efficiencies on the demand side (energy consumption). That being the case, I would like to express my gratitude to the following individuals for generously sharing their time with me:

For reasons of marital harmony and because of the hours semi-willingly committed to early drafts, my wife Amie (ex-lawyer and committed campaigner for sound causes). Also: Brian Matthews for some quite brilliant photography; Harry Boyd-Carpenter for sharing his thoughts on global investment issues; Chris Davies for his unparalled experience of the coal, gas and nuclear industry; Chris Train for his unique perspectives on the networks and the possibilities for decarbonised gas (including hydrogen); Clare Jackson for sharing her views on the growing hydrogen sector; Will Collins on the challenges facing onshore, offshore and island wind developers; Phil Davies on the early promise of one of the UK's pilot carbon capture and use projects; Mark Hollands for his perspectives on the investment challenges for onshore developers in a post-subsidy world; Nigel Knee as all round policy guru; Matilda Le Prevost for some sound common sense; Richard Deakin for sharing views in a personal capacity on the potential pathways for advanced nuclear; Tom Palmer for finding time in a very hectic schedule to share thoughts on what comes next; and, also, each of the publications referred to in the report who kindly let me use their charts and figures. Thanks also to my supportive team at Fieldfisher for giving me the space to write the report (and particularly my IP consultant Abigail Cannon).

I. Introduction

Pour ce qui est de l'avenir, il ne s'agit pas de le prévoir, mais de le rendre possible?
Antoine de Saint Exupéry, *Citadelle*, 1948[1]

The second half of 2019 saw an unprecedented level of public interest in the implications of rising global greenhouse gas emissions (GHGEs). In the UK, this coincided with the government's decision to legislate for Net Zero by 2050, which meant that all GHGEs must be eliminated entirely by 2050 (previously the target was an 80% reduction relative to 1990 levels). This is a remarkable commitment and Net Zero become a central aspect of the December 2019 general election campaign, shaded only by the ongoing Brexit debate. Many towns, airports and private companies have adopted their own Net Zero ambitions at significantly earlier timescales (2030 being a recurring favourite).

The scale of change required to deliver Net Zero should not be underestimated. It will require a wholesale disruption not just to the functioning of energy systems and commercial industries, but in individual behaviour and personal lives. It will entail the abolition of all non-electric cars by 2040 (and probably much earlier), a significant increase in the electrification of energy supply, the decarbonisation of natural gas, electric and hybrid heating systems, fundamental improvements to energy efficiency, new approaches to land use and considerably changed personal diets and travel behaviour.

Power generation is at the vanguard of the road to Net Zero. The UK's electricity mix is currently around 45% renewable power (by capacity, lower by actual output). This rises to 53% 'low carbon' once nuclear capacity is added. To get anywhere close to 100% carbon-free will require investment in wind, solar, nuclear, energy storage, hydrogen and carbon capture and storage (CCS) technology at an unprecedented scale over the next 30 years. The growth required in this sector will far exceed the level of investment to date under a number of very generous renewable technology support schemes. Most of those schemes have now closed to new projects, which underscores the scale of the challenge ahead.

This Special Report explores a number of themes arising from the need to decarbonise electricity generation and to electrify more of our energy consumption. Chapters II and III explore the existing levels of investment in renewable power generation across the world and in the UK, and the impact this is having, both on the cost of renewable projects and on GHGEs. It explains the power generation mix in the UK, and why there is a difference between the installed capacity of

"The scale of change required to deliver Net Zero will require a wholescale disruption not just to the functioning of energy systems and commercial industries, but in individual behaviour and personal lives."

any given technology and its actual electrical output. Chapter IV looks at the development of UK energy policy over the last 20 years, including renewable energy subsidy schemes, and the emergence and implications of Net Zero. Chapters V and VI give an overview of our main generation technologies, moving from conventional to renewable forms of power. Chapter VII concludes by looking at the emergence of the new technologies that will be required to deliver Net Zero (eg, energy storage, floating wind, hydrogen, carbon capture and small nuclear). Finally, chapter VIII explains how the UK electricity system works and how the National Grid maintains the continuous real-time balance of electricity supply and demand (and so, how blackouts occur).

This report will appeal to those who are new to, or work in, the energy industry, particularly those involved in power generation activities. Although its primary focus is the decarbonisation of electricity and the greater electrification of energy consumption, it will also be of interest to those who are concerned with the Net Zero agenda and want to understand the implications of this radical new ambition on the energy system as a whole. It has been written with both the lawyer and non-lawyer in mind, and should provide an indispensable introduction to today's most pressing energy-related issues.

Amongst other things, this report addresses the following questions:

- How important is renewable technology to global and UK energy supply?
- Have renewable energy projects been successful in curtailing rising and harmful levels of GHGEs?
- What is the Paris Agreement and Net Zero policy, where did they come from and what steps will be required to deliver those ambitions? How realistic is the scale of transformation required to limit global warming to 2°C?
- What are the main generation technologies in the UK and how do they work?
- What are the main policy factors affecting energy generation projects and what issues arise from the need to invest in renewable technology?
- What new technologies will be required to deliver Net Zero?
- What is the UK electricity grid and how does National Grid balance supply and demand?

II. The global energy triumvirate: greenhouse gas emissions, global warming and green energy

1. Global energy trends – overview

This chapter considers the issue of decarbonising energy by looking at the extent to which the global power sector reflects the new low-carbon ambitions. The benchmark for those ambitions is contained in the remarkable Paris Agreement (2015) consensus to keep the average global temperature rise this century "well below" 2°C above pre-industrial levels and to "endeavour to limit" it even further, to 1.5°C. The scale of that challenge, and the urgency of a coordinated response, is underscored by the recent announcement that we have already reached approximately 1°C of warming over pre-industrial levels.

The consequences of exceeding these targets are sobering. The Intergovernmental Panel on Climate Change (IPCC) believes that limiting global warming to 1.5°C is expected to "substantially reduce the probability of extreme drought, precipitation deficits, and risks associated with water availability". These effects are already being observed at the current 1°C level of warming. The IPCC also believes that "exposure to multiple and compound climate-related risks is projected to increase between 1.5°C and 2°C of global warming".[2]

Within that context, decarbonising the energy sector is of fundamental importance (the power sector is the largest source of carbon emissions).

The challenge of summarising progress towards decarbonising global energy is attributable to the sheer scale and complexity of the global energy market. This is exacerbated by the sometimes kinetosis-inducing speed of change; a constant motion of peaks and troughs of different sorts dominating headlines at any one moment. Nonetheless, some broad trends have emerged from the past decade, and that is despite the continuous publication of new policy and legislation, daily announcements of technology breakthroughs, tumbling costs and exciting new markets. This chapter draws out the following three key themes:

- Global emissions of greenhouses gasses have not stabilised, but continue to rise at a significant rate. Nonetheless, the reality of human-induced climate change is now more deeply recognised than ever before, and there is growing pressure on governments, multinationals and corporates to curtail emissions and promote decarbonisation.
- In parallel, global investment in renewable capacity has risen to remarkable levels. Renewable technology is widely recognised as allowing the decarbonisation of electricity supply cheaply and at scale. This allows activities that are carbon-intensive or otherwise pollutive (transport, industrial processes, heating) to switch to low-carbon electricity, which promotes the electrification of our primary energy use (primary energy use considers our consumption of energy from all fuel types – eg, petrol in a car or natural gas in a domestic boiler).
- With investment rising, the cost of renewable technologies is rapidly decreasing, and in fact in many countries it is now the most cost-competitive form of power generation.

The scale of the transformation required to achieve the ambition of the Paris Agreement is titanic. The message of this chapter is perhaps best captured like this: in the crow's nest and on the decks, the iceberg of irreversible climate damage has just emerged from the fog, but although the engine room has responded to the cries on deck, the boat is a large one and takes a long time to turn. As things stand, it looks like the cries have come too late and some sort of impact will ensue; hopefully only a glancing one. That future, at first murky and indistinct, is now taking shape as it looms ever closer. The question for those of us on board is: How will we choose to respond? The lifeboats of complacency have a sad echo in history.

2. Green shoots still to bud: carbon far from dated

2.1 The coal problem

There exists a 'good news/bad news' dilemma when it comes to weighing up the success of efforts to decarbonise global electricity generation. Although more solar capacity has been installed during the last decade than any other type of generating technology, coal was still second, with an additional 529 gigawatts (GW) of coal plants added worldwide. This means that although electricity generation is rising globally, coal power generation still provides the same contribution as renewables to this increase (both around a third).

While the renewables share of total power generation increased from 8.4% to 9.3% in 2018 (in Europe it is more like 19%), coal still had the largest share of overall power generation at 38%.[3] Remarkably, despite all the investment in renewables, that incumbent coal figure is largely unchanged over the last three decades (in 1990 it was 37%). In principle, the coal plants could be cleaned up, including through effective sulphur dioxide, nitrogen oxide and dust abatement, and retrofitting with carbon capture, use and storage technology (CCUS). However, CCUS would involve very expensive upgrade works and it is hard to see where the global incentive to do so would come from, with industry costs already being high and generators having to tolerate low market prices and minimal margins. The only clear method of achieving the required cleanup is with a strong carbon price to reflect the true cost of carbon emissions, on the 'polluter pays' principle. Alternatives to CCUS include retrofitting coal plants with biomass

Figure 1: Growth in power generation, showing the strong growth in renewables and coal

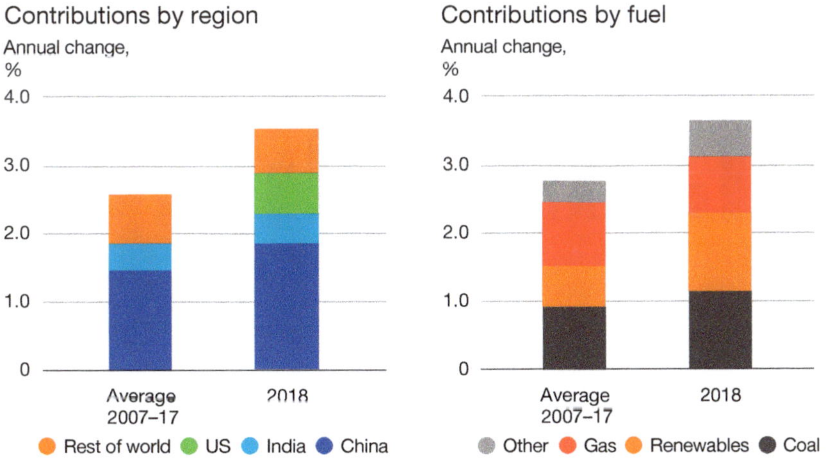

Source: © BP Statistical Review of World Energy 2019

co-firing equipment, repurposing them to focus on network support and flexibility, or retiring them early in favour of renewable technology. All look unlikely in the context of the rapidly growing energy needs of China, India and other emerging economies.

2.2 Global greenhouse gas emissions (GHGEs) and global warming

The existing global fleet of fossil fuelled power stations and the new additions over the last decade mean that carbon emissions from the global power sector are likely to have risen by around 11% over the decade.[4] That is despite the Paris Agreement commitments outlined in section 1 above. The importance of securing this average temperature outcome has been emphasised in two further reports from the IPCC in 2019, both of which articulate fundamental concerns about observed and potential climate change events.[5]

It might be too early to say whether the global trend of rising GHGEs over the decade has started to turn, with a mixed picture emerging in the last couple of years. Analysis of GHGEs on 2018 figures suggests the existing direction of travel does not appear to be changing, as captured in BP's Statistical Review of Energy (2019)[6] and the UN's Emissions Gap Report (2019).[7] BP's report observed that both global energy demand and carbon emissions from energy use (this is from

Figure 2: Carbon emissions from the power sector

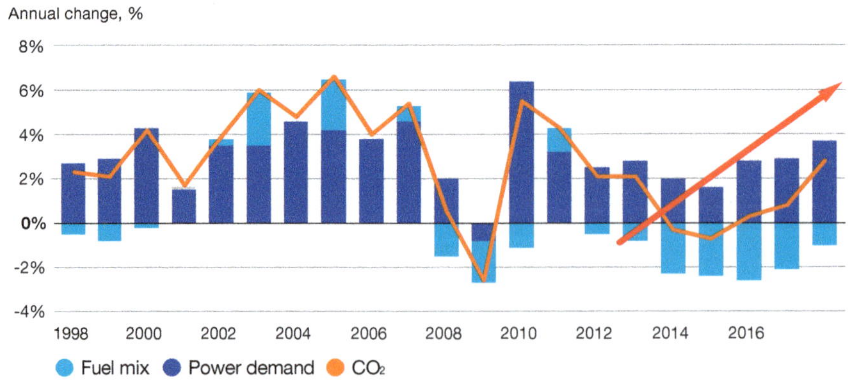

Source: © BP Statistical Review of World Energy 2019

the total consumption of energy) grew in 2018 at their fastest rate since 2010/11, leading to an associated increase in carbon emissions of 2% (half of which is attributable to the power sector). BP claims that this 2% rise in carbon emissions is equivalent to increasing the number of passenger cars on the planet by a third.

Coming after BP's report, the most recent UN Emissions Gap report (published in November 2019) does not provide comfortable reading. The purpose of the report is to compare the level of actual GHGEs with the actions that would be required to deliver the agreed climate goals. That report found that not only have global GHGEs failed to decline, they are not even slowing down. It concluded that emissions have continued to rise steadily (at an average rate of 1.5% per year in the last decade), hitting a new high of 55.3 gigatonnes of CO2 equivalent in 2018. Worryingly, this means we are on course for a 3.2°C temperature rise by the end of the century. The UN believes that the continuing rise in GHGEs has made the Paris Agreement 1.5°C target increasingly unrealistic (it would require a 7.6% drop in emissions each year to 2030) and that on current trends even the 2°C target will not be met unless there is at least a 2.7% drop in emissions each year to 2030. As things stand, the UN sees little to even indicate that GHGEs will peak in the next few years – and each year that passes

Figure 3: Rising global GHGEs over the last two decades

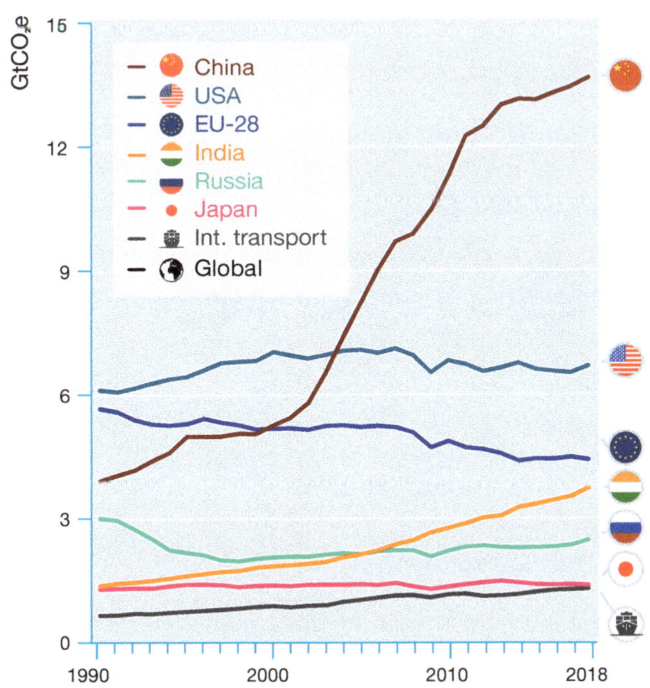

Source: © United Nations Environment Programme (2019) Emissions Gap Report 2019, UNEP, Nairobi

makes the goal harder to reach, requiring ever more urgent and drastic reductions. The conclusions of the UN's report echo those of the International Energy Agency (IEA), which points to the "ever-higher amounts of GHGEs being produced and the insufficiency of stated policies to curb those emissions in line with international climate targets".[8]

Even on the basis of countries meeting their existing pledges, the UN forecasts that GHGEs will continue to rise and, by 2030, GHGEs may be 27% and 38% higher than the level needed to limit warming to 2°C and 1.5°C respectively.[9] The IEA reaches a similar conclusion, noting in its Stated Policies Scenario, which projects the consequences of implementing existing policy intentions and targets, that not enough has been done to avoid the worst impacts of climate change. It points out that "momentum behind clean energy is insufficient to offset the effects of an expanding global economy and growing population. The rise in emissions in this scenario slows but does not peak before 2040." Successfully delivering the Paris Agreement target (under its Sustainable Development Scenario) would require rapid and widespread changes across all parts of the energy system, including sharp emission cuts through the use of multiple fuels and technologies.

Figure 4: Global GHGEs under different scenarios and the emissions gap by 2030

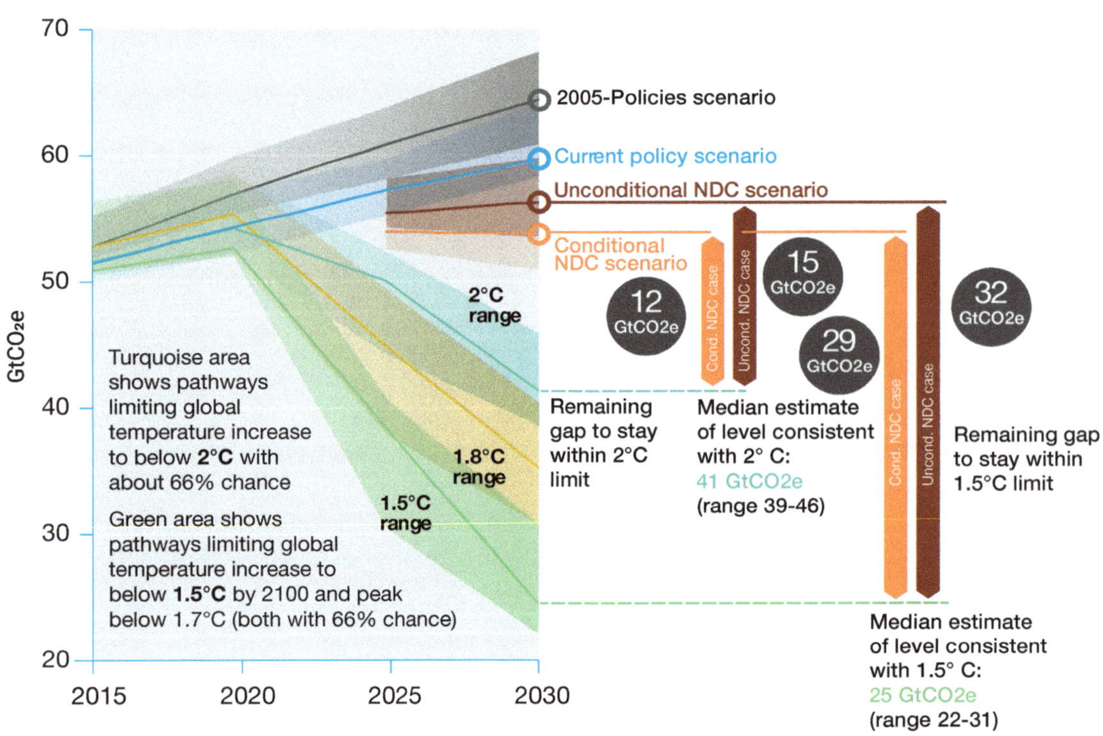

Source: © United Nations Environment Programme (2019) Emissions Gap Report 2019, UNEP, Nairobi

Although 65 countries have made Net Zero commitments, that number only includes five of the G20 group (the G20 members account for 78% of GHGEs) and only two of those, the UK and France, have introduced binding legislation to deliver that target. The key conclusion of the UN's report is that there remains an unacceptably large gap between what countries have committed to achieve on GHGE reductions and the actions that would be required to meet the Paris Agreement targets (and that assumes countries actually deliver on their existing commitments). On top of that, several major economies, including the United States, Canada, Australia, Japan and Brazil, are already well off meeting their Paris Agreement Nationally Determined Contributions (NDCs). This growing gap between GHGEs and reaching the Paris Agreement target is demonstrated in Figure 4.

DNV GL also released a report in 2019 that forecast the 2°C ambition will be missed (on current polices), predicting global energy-related emissions will only peak in 2025. That report projects a levelling off in global energy demand after 2030, when energy efficiency improvements start to outpace economic growth. An even starker projection has recently come out from the US Energy Information Administration, which forecasts an almost 50% rise in world energy use by 2050 and a massive 79% increase in electricity generation (in both cases from 2018) as a result of increased electricity consumption in all end-user sectors.[10]

Those forecasts based on trends up to and including 2018 may, hopefully, be moderated by updated figures published by the IEA in February 2020 which demonstrate that, contrary to widespread expectations, global energy-related CO_2 emissions actually flattened in 2019, and power-related emissions of advanced economies fell sharply (www.iea.org/articles/global-co2-emissions-in-2019). The IEA attributes this surprising departure from historic global emissions growth to a combination of:

- expanding output of renewable sources;
- fuel switching from coal to natural gas; and
- higher nuclear power output.

It is also likely that milder weather and weaker global economic growth over 2019 played an important role. What remains to be seen, however, is whether (to quote the IEA in its accompanying press release) 2019 comes to be regarded as the "definitive peak in global emissions, not just another pause in growth".

It is difficult to be too precise about the underlying factors behind the continuing growth in power-related emissions over the past decade (whether or not arrested in 2019). Population and economic growth in emerging economies are obviously factors but BP's report also notes that there were an unusually large number of hot and cold days in 2018, so possibly weather patterns resulted in an increase in demand for heating and cooling over the year (both very energy-intensive processes). The IPCC reports referred to in sections 1 and 2.2 above also identify an increasing frequency and intensity of climate events. But the milder weather in 2019 has also been associated with the flattened global energy-related emissions for that year. It therefore remains to be seen how much variable weather patterns will drive the future demand of energy and its associated emissions. Whatever the explanation, unchecked rising consumption is manifestly unsustainable from a global policy perspective, for the longer carbon emissions continue to rise, the harder and more expensive will be the adjustment required to get anywhere near the Paris Agreement ambition (at least for so long as unabated fossil fuels dominate energy use).

3. Global green energy: an investment success story?

3.1 Investment in renewables

In the context of rising GHGEs and serious concerns over the deliverability of the Paris Agreement, the level of investment in renewable power generation becomes very important (as it is the primary pathway to decarbonising electricity). There are reasons to promote and invest in renewable power beyond simply its relationship with securing international climate targets:

- It avoids local pollution.
- It is cost-competitive or even cheaper than conventional forms of generation.
- It offers energy security (no dependency on imported oil or gas).
- It offers price stability (being fuel-free it is not linked to international gas or oil prices).

Perhaps more than anything else though, renewable power facilitates two things: the decarbonisation of electricity cheaply and at scale and, consequently, the increased electrification of energy use. This is discussed in more detail in section 3.5 below. On this basis, there is cause for considerable optimism. Over the decade to the end of 2019, there has been a massive US$2.6 trillion invested in renewable energy capacity.[11] That is more than treble the amount of the previous decade. The significant benefactor of this has been photovoltaic (PV) solar (referred to in this report just as solar),[12] which accounted for over half of global spend (US$1.3 trillion). Solar was closely followed by wind (41%, about US$1 trillion), with biomass and energy from waste (EfW) some way behind at US$115 billion. Biomass involves the use of organic fuels (eg, wood pellets) in thermal generation and EfW uses refuse that would otherwise go to landfill. The choice of technology is crucial in driving the

Figure 5: Global capacity in renewable power, 2004–2018, gigawatts (GW)

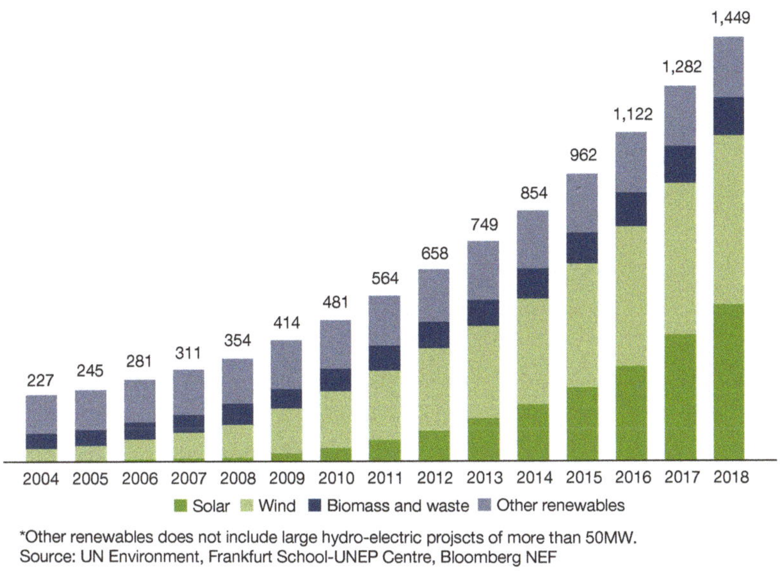

Source: © UN and BloombergNEF's Global Trends in Renewable Energy Investment 2019

transition to low-carbon generation, and it is extremely positive that global investment in renewable capacity in 2018 was about three times that of investment in coal- and gas-fired generation capacity combined.[13]

China was, by some way, the leader in renewable capacity investment over this period, accounting for around 31% of global spend.[14] The second highest spender, the US, was somewhat surprisingly quite far behind, spending about half the amount China did. Europe as a whole invested US$698 billion (which was 28% of the total, so still less than China), with Germany and the UK the biggest spenders. Nonetheless, global investment in new renewable capacity in 2018 dropped 12% from 2017. The reason for this fall was a steep deceleration in solar investment, mostly attributable to a downturn in solar financings in China (due to the unforeseen withdrawal of Feed-in Tariffs (FiT)) and the lower average capital costs per megawatt (MW) for both wind and solar in most economies.

3.2 Growing capacity

From a global perspective and notwithstanding the financial cooling in 2018, investment in solar has been a remarkable success. Global developers installed more solar capacity during the last decade than any other form of generating technology (fossil or renewable). A remarkable 638GW of solar capacity was installed, utterly transforming the sector from its mere 25GW of capacity worldwide in 2009.[15] Not far behind, onshore wind capacity increased four times over the decade, and offshore wind by a factor of 15. In fact, global offshore wind grew nearly 30% per year between 2010 and 2018 (and, going forwards, Europe is anticipated to quadruple its capacity by 2030). Yet the IEA believes this is only a drop in the ocean of global offshore wind's full potential, which could (with appropriate policy support) have the capability to deliver more than 18 times global electricity demand today (that would be about 420,000 terawatt-hour (TWh) per year worldwide).[16]

Natural gas, although by no means a low-carbon technology, is preferable to coal and oil/diesel as it is a considerably less carbon-intensive form of generation. BP's 2019 Statistical Review found that natural gas consumption grew in 2018 at one of its fastest rates for over 30 years (largely driven by US shale gas), accounting for over 40% of the growth in primary energy use.[17] Renewable power generation (mainly wind and solar) also continued to grow far more rapidly in 2018 than any other form of energy (up by 14.5%, which was slightly below its historical average). And, as was true of the decade as a whole, China was the largest contributor to renewables growth in 2018 (claiming 45% of global growth in renewable power generation).

This bias in favour of renewable capacity investment has come at a remarkable speed. At the start of 2010, wind and solar accounted for only 4% of the world's generating capacity (and much less of the electricity actually produced from the capacity). At that time, renewables technology was almost derisorily regarded as expensive and niche, not to mention being entirely dependent on public subsidies to be investable. Similarly, the importance of a strong carbon price to reflect the pollutive and greenhouse gas (GHG) consequences of fossil fuel power was not widely accepted. However, by the end of the decade, wind and solar technology accounted for 18% of global generating capacity, a really quite remarkable growth story.[18]

Figure 6 illustrates DNV GL's forecasted decline in the fossil fuel share of the primary energy supply mix from around 81% today to 56% by 2050.

3.3 Back to the future (again)

The success of investment in renewable capacity is a trend that looks set to continue. After the 2018 cooling mentioned at the end of section 3.1 above, global annual capacity growth is forecast to have resumed in 2019. Accelerating growth in the US, Europe and the Asia-Pacific region is likely to have offset the flatter growth in China. A report by the IEA outlines that renewable power capacity is set to grow by 50% between 2019 and 2024.[19] This 1,200GW increase (from 2,502GW in 2018) is led by solar (accounting for almost 60% of the increase) with onshore wind

Figure 6: World primary energy supply by source (forecast to 2050)

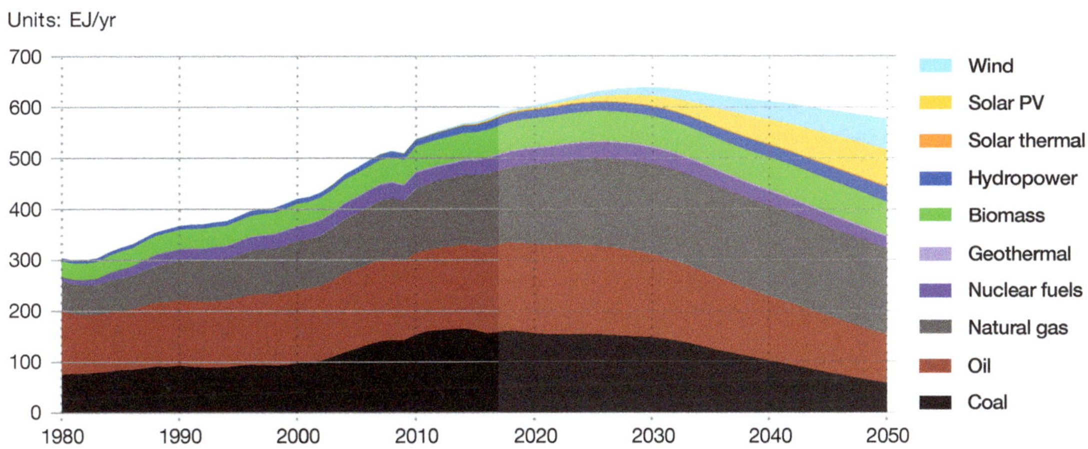

Source: © DNV GL Energy Transition Outlook 2019

contributing about 25%, and offshore wind and biomass both around 4% of the increase (this still corresponds to a tripling of offshore wind's existing capacity). A capacity rise of 1,200GW is very significant – the IEA point out it is equivalent to the total installed power capacity of the US today. The rise could be higher still if governments overcome the three investment challenges of regulatory uncertainty, investment risks in developing countries and system integration of wind and solar generation.

3.4 Capacity is not power

It is important to bear in mind the incomplete congruence between the growing capacity (in megawatts (MW)) of newly installed wind and solar projects and the actual amount of electricity (in megawatt-hours (MWh)) that is generated from them (ie, their utilisation). The 'capacity factor' of wind and solar technology is a reflection that their installed capacity does not stack up well against their share of electricity actually generated. Global capacity factors of solar are in the 11–35% range due to sunlight dependency, whereas coal is in principle only constrained by maintenance outages and unfavourable market prices when renewable output is high. Fortunately, this gap is narrowing for most renewable technologies. One interesting consequence of the growth of the offshore wind sector is that larger and more distant offshore turbines are able to access stronger and more regular wind flows. This means they can achieve lower variability of output (ie, lower intermittency), which prompted the IEA to categorise them as "the only variable baseload power generation technology", achieving average capacity factors of around of 40–50%.[20]

3.5 Electrifying energy

The growing investment in renewable technology has helped contribute towards the increasing electrification of the global energy market. This means, as a factor of total energy use, more and more energy is being consumed as electricity. In 2018, power demand (that is, the demand for electricity produced through power generation) increased more strongly than overall energy demand, as the world started to electrify more of its energy consumption. This trend will grow even stronger if the anticipated widespread electrification of heat and transport proves correct. A report by DNV GL concluded that electrification, primarily driven by renewable sources, will be the biggest contributor to reduced energy intensity (and therefore reduced emissions).[21] In fact, that report predicts the share of electricity in final energy consumption will more than double over the next 30 years: from a rather modest 19% today to 40% in 2050, two thirds of which will be generated by wind and solar. DNV GL predict that in 2050, renewable power will provide almost 80% of the electricity mix, and be much more geographically dispersed. Nonetheless, that still means the majority of energy consumption is not provided through electricity, which means renewables will not be able to dominate energy supply.

Similarly, the US Energy Information Administration forecasts that although renewable energy will be the world's fastest growing form of energy, it is only expected to supply around 28% of global primary energy consumption by 2050. This means that renewable generation will still lag behind fossil fuels as a share of primary energy consumption in 2050.[22] These reports do not necessarily mean, however, that other forms of low-carbon fuels cannot be developed to complement electricity, such as hydrogen. Hydrogen is discussed in greater detail in chapter VII.

The IEA, in its World Energy Outlook 2019, also sees electricity use growing at more than double the pace of overall energy demand in its Stated Policies Scenario. Growth in electricity use here is driven by industrial motors (particularly in China), household appliances, cooling and electric vehicles (EVs). The continuing growth in wind and solar generation means renewables are set to overtake coal in the power generation mix at some point in the mid-2020s. The IEA believes that by 2040, low-carbon sources will provide more than half of total electricity generation (which is a landmark the UK reached in 2019, as set out in chapter III). In the IEA's Sustainable Development Scenario, the share of electricity in final energy consumption, being less than half that of oil today, overtakes oil by 2040.

Figure 7: World electricity generation by power station type

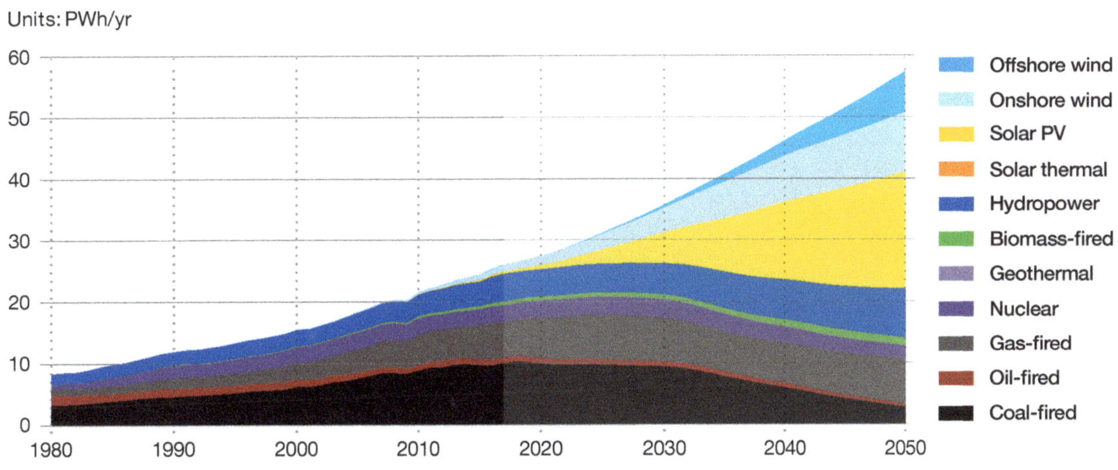

Source: © DNV GL Energy Transition Outlook 2019

4. Renewable technology: now cheaper and more efficient

4.1 Falling costs

Considering the relatively recent perception of renewable technology as being expensive and dependent on public subsidy, it is incredible that renewable projects are now amongst the cheapest source of new power generation in many parts of the world.

Since 2010, the global-weighted average levelised cost of energy (LCOE) from bioenergy (which includes biomass and biogas), hydropower, geothermal, onshore wind and offshore wind have been within the price range of fossil fuel power generation.[23] In 2014, the global-weighted average LCOE of solar also fell into the fossil fuel price range. This relative parity was driven by a spectacular improvement in the cost-competitiveness of renewables: the LCOE for solar came down 81% over the decade (to US$57/MWh); onshore wind came down 46% (US$50) and offshore wind came down 44% (to US$89/MWh).

Figure 8: Levelised cost of electricity (LCOE), by main renewable energy technology, 2009 to 2019, US$/MWh

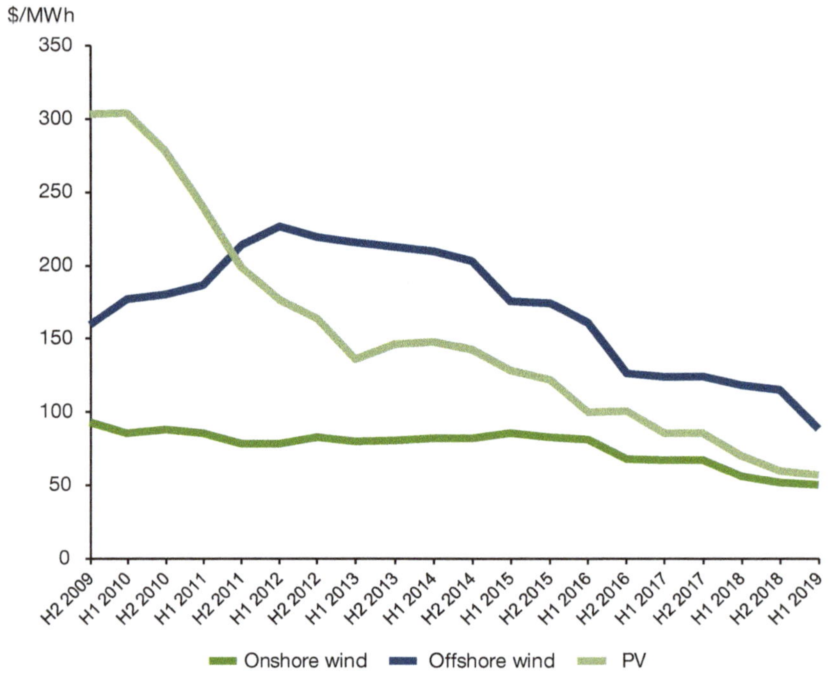

Source: © UN & Bloomberg NEF's Global Trends in Renewable Energy Investment 2019

By 2020, onshore wind and solar are anticipated to have moved beyond the fossil fuel price range to become a cheaper source of electricity than the least-cost fossil fuel alternative (which means they would cost less than the marginal operating cost of existing coal plants). Offshore wind will continue to fall but will probably remain in the top half of the fossil fuel price range for a while. The recalibration of renewable technology cost competitiveness shows how quickly the landscape has changed. This means that renewable energy projects, in principle, do not need additional public subsidy to make them competitive with fossil fuel generation. In fact, many developing economies avoided the mistake of creating a green subsidy dependency by moving straight to competition through renewable technology auctions alone.

As it happened, the consequence of generous subsidies in developed economies was unforeseen levels of private sector investment, leading to concerns over the larger than estimated impact on consumer bills. There was accordingly a rather rapid rewriting of the subsidy dynamic in several economies, including the unceremoniously swift closure of the FiT and Renewables Obligation (RO) schemes in the UK (the same happened in China in 2018). Auctioning renewable capacity is now more widely regarded as the most economically efficient means of

Figure 9: Falling cost of solar and wind generation (2010–18)

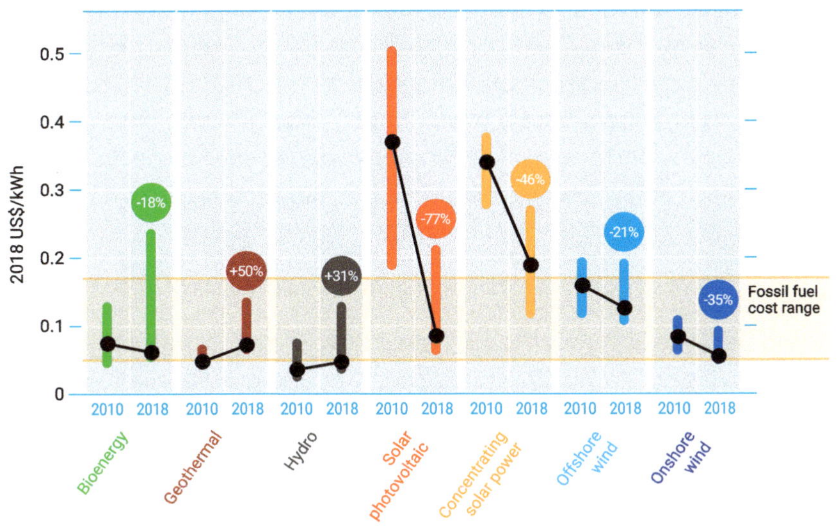

Source: © United Nations Environment Programme (2019) Emissions Gap Report 2019, UNEP, Nairobi

procuring the additional capacity at the lowest practicable cost – as in the UK with the Contracts for Difference (CfD) regime and, to a more modest extent, the Capacity Market (CM). See chapters IV and VI for a discussion of these schemes.

4.2 Explaining the cost savings

Several factors have contributed towards the growing cost competiveness of renewable generation. They include:

(a) Competition in supply

As mentioned in section 4.1 above, procurement auctions over direct subsidies have been increasingly influential in driving price competition. The growth of the renewable sector more generally has also led to much more competitive global supply chains (particularly in China).

(b) Manufacturing economies of scale

The size of individual wind and solar farms has trended upwards over time, as developers react to cheaper finance, proven technology and the possibility of bigger project footprints when local conditions allow. The emergence of these larger projects facilitates cost savings through economies of scale in the manufacturing and development stages.

(c) Operation and maintenance (O&M) economies of scale
Similar to point (b), as project sizes have increased in scale, there have been more opportunities to find significant cost savings in the operating phase. For example, one O&M contractor can be retained to perform all O&M services for a cluster of offshore wind farms (rather than having different O&M providers for each wind farm). Similarly, the emergence of larger turbines, better use of technology (eg, remote inspection through drones) and more reliable predictive fault management have all helped to bring down the 'per Megawatt' cost of O&M.

(d) Geographical optimisation
Solar and offshore wind farms are increasingly being developed in regions with higher capacity factors (eg, Africa and Australia for solar developments, and far-offshore for wind farms where turbines can access higher and more regular wind flows).

(e) Technological optimisation
Similar to geographical optimisation, continued investment in research and development (R&D) means developers now have a wider range of technologies to select from to optimise the climatic conditions of the specific project location. This also helps minimise the LCOE for wind power across a range of operating conditions.

(f) Technological improvements
There have been continued technological improvements in the efficiency of wind turbines and solar panels (eg, bifacial panels and solar tracking mountings). These improvements have allowed more MWh of energy to be generated from the same MW of capacity, which is why offshore wind farms have an apparent advantage over onshore projects: they can generate more output from fewer turbines.

(g) Favourable public policy
Generally, governmental policy has been to promote investment in renewable technology. At best, this takes the form of direct subsidy support of renewable projects but it also captures carbon-prejudicial legislation and inter-governmental commitments to low-carbon targets. Introducing a stable revenue source (for subsidised generation) and bringing down the regulatory and political risk of investing in low-carbon technologies all helps cultivate an attractive investment environment.

(h) Cheaper financing costs
The falling cost of capital (being the cost of raising finance for a project) has been particularly important for renewable projects because of their front-ended spend profile. They require significant upfront capital expenditure but have comparatively low ongoing running costs (and no fuel costs). As such, the cost of equity and

debt in financing new projects has become very influential in the calculation of their total LCOE. By way of example, the total cost of debt for a German onshore wind farm dropped from 6% in 2009 to 2.2 % in early 2018.[24] Relatedly, record low interest rates in major economies over the decade has created competition between investors and banks to participate in renewable energy projects; all good news for developers looking to raise finance for their projects.

4.3 Price competition and the path to diminishing marginal returns

The upshot of this decade of rigorous price competition is that, by the early 2020s, all available renewable power generation options will compete head to head with the fossil incumbents, and renewable technology will become the cheapest option in many countries. Looking further ahead, the DNV GL report predicts solar costs will drop to less than 60% of today's levels by 2050. Other estimates have it as much as 80%. It is not all good news for renewable project developers though, as the high penetration of intermittent renewable generation leads to weaker power prices for wind and solar when competing between themselves. This is because when it is particularly windy or sunny, all available wind or solar produces at available capacity, leading to a phenomenon known as wholesale price cannibalisation (explored in greater detail in chapter VI).[25]

"The upshot of this decade of rigorous price competition is that, by the early 2020s, all available renewable power generation options will compete head to head with the fossil incumbents, and renewable technology will become the cheapest option in many countries."

Alongside price cannibalisation, there is a second cost implication of the renewables success story. With the growing penetration of renewable generation, it becomes increasingly important to look beyond the marginal cost of a particular technology to the total system costs (which are the additional costs associated with incorporating a particular technology into the electricity system). Incidents of renewable technology exacerbating existing system costs are already emerging in mature electricity markets. For example, in the UK the growing proportion of intermittent wind and solar generation exporting onto the grid at relatively short notice has been associated with a number of stability issues. These can range widely, from the gradual loss of system inertia (traditionally provided by the spinning turbines of thermal plants) to National Grid's need to have a broader range of tools at its disposal to manage system frequency and reserve power. Perhaps more so than any other generation characteristic, flexibility is becoming the watchword of global electricity systems (see chapter VIII for a discussion of these topics).

Similar to these price observations, diminishing marginal returns on renewable penetration means we cannot extrapolate a nice clear line to a 100% renewable energy sector. Renewable generation, being fuel-free, does not allow for an easy correlation of supply and demand, meaning there are likely to be significant periods where demand is high but renewable output is low, so other forms of fuelled generation and energy storage will be required. Conversely, where there is an oversupply of renewable energy, the power may objectively be cheap but it is also worth less as a commodity because supply has exceeded demand at that point, often leading to generation being curtailed. These intermittency-driven spikes will eventually be moderated by short-term (eg, lithium-ion battery) and long-term (eg, compressed hydrogen or ammonia) storage and by more sophisticated demand response/shifting, as well as greater interconnectedness between energy markets. We are only in the early stages of these developments and they are picked up later in the report. To an extent though, they are regarded as good problems to have.

A second driver of diminishing marginal returns is the limited availability of appropriate sites. Renewable generation requires access to the best renewable resources – being both the land the technology is located on and high, regular levels of available sun or wind (as well as proximity to a place of demand or connection point to the local energy network). The best sites tend to be used first, meaning the costs of accessing subsequent sites may actually become more expensive rather than cheaper. To an extent, this is being seen in the North Sea with offshore wind developers starting to look at floating wind technology as a means of accessing better wind

"If the seeds of optimism are to be found anywhere, it is in the fact that unsubsidised renewable technology is now price competitive with incumbent fossil fuel technology and that an increasing number of countries, corporates and regions have started to prioritise climate change as a major (or even the number one) political issue."

resources. The cost of moving 'properly' offshore is obviously higher (at least initially) and carries with it a new level of logistical challenge to traditional seabed-mounted turbines.

5. Global wrap-up

What conclusions can be reached from the apparent inconsistency between the considerable investment in renewable forms of generation (as the proxy for decarbonising electricity) and the contemporaneous growth in power-related GHGEs? It is clear that the rapid gains in renewable energy have not been sufficient to offset the pace of growth in power demand, meaning that overall carbon emissions from the power sector have continued to rise. In a nutshell, decarbonisation of the power sector has not happened fast enough to offset the continued growth in demand for power. Rather worryingly, the BP report suggests that renewable power should have grown more than twice as quickly as it actually did in order to maintain carbon emissions from the power sector at their 2015 level (1800TWh versus actual growth of 800TWh). This 'missing capacity' is roughly equivalent to the entire renewable generation of China and the US combined in 2018. It remains to be seen, though, whether the unexpected stabilisation of energy-related emissions in 2019 will represent the peak or simply a pause in their growth (of which there have been several over the past two decades).

Along with decreasing demand through energy efficiency measures, it is only really the electrification of energy consumption that provides a credible pathway to a less carbon-intensive energy system, but only if the power sector itself becomes almost entirely decarbonised. As BP's report pithily puts it: "Electrification without decarbonizing power is of little use". If the seeds of optimism are to be found anywhere, it is in the fact that unsubsidised renewable technology is now price competitive with incumbent fossil fuel technology and that an increasing number of countries, corporates and regions have started to prioritise climate change as a major (or even the number one) political issue.

With an appropriate level of public support and the continued cooperation of governments towards a common goal, the cost competitiveness of renewable technology should see an exponential impact on GHGEs stabilisation. The challenge will be bringing this about in a timescale that makes meeting the Paris Agreement remotely achievable, and this is where the concern really lies. It is abundantly clear that there is no silver bullet in defeating climate change and harnessing global temperature rises. At the heart of most strategies are the following, all discussed in further detail elsewhere in this report:

- far higher energy efficiency at all levels (domestic, industrial and commercial);
- considerably more renewable power generation;
- the electrification of heat and transport; and
- the decarbonisation of gas through a shift to hydrogen and/or the development of industrial-scale CCUS.

III. How green is UK energy?

1. UK energy trends – overview

Chapter II examined three things: growing investment in renewable projects globally; falling costs of renewable technology; and the fact that despite the growing investment in renewable technology, GHGEs are still rising. This chapter takes a slightly different approach by looking more closely at the composition of the generation mix in the UK, and how well the UK is progressing in its own transition to a decarbonised power sector. The 'generation mix' is the respective contribution of each form of power-generating technology (coal, nuclear, gas, wind etc) to creating electricity that is then dispatched to industrial, commercial and domestic customers.

The year 2019 was a watershed for clean energy in the UK as, for the first time, the amount of zero-carbon power supply outstripped that of fossil fuels: 48.5% of the UK's energy was provided by a combination of wind and solar farms, nuclear energy and subsea interconnectors. By comparison, 43% of electricity was generated by fossil fuels. The rest was provided by biomass.[26]

There is an important distinction between how much a given technology contributes to generating electricity (this refers to its output, measured in megawatt-hours (MWh) or gigawatt-hours (GWh)) and how much of a given type of technology there is available on the system (this refers to its installed capacity, measured in megawatts (MW) or gigawatts (GW). In discussions on the energy mix, it is common to express both as a percentage – either of total electricity generated over a period (for output) or of the capacity installed at a point in time (for capacity), and it is surprisingly easy to mix up the figures. The distinction has relevance. For example, wind power makes up a reasonable proportion of the UK's installed generating capacity, but on a particularly still day its level of generated electricity will be very low.[27]

2. Energy versus electricity

As explained in chapter II, electricity generation and consumption is just one form of energy use – and it is rather surprisingly a minority one. In the UK, electricity consumption accounts for only about 17% of final energy consumption (other obvious examples of energy consumption are petrol in vehicles and natural gas to heat residential and office space). Figure 10 illustrates the respective importance of different sources of energy in meeting the UK's needs (figures are expressed in million tonnes oil equivalent (mtoe)). As can be seen, fossil fuels (particularly petroleum and natural gas) still dominate.

Figure 10: Summary of UK energy flows 2018

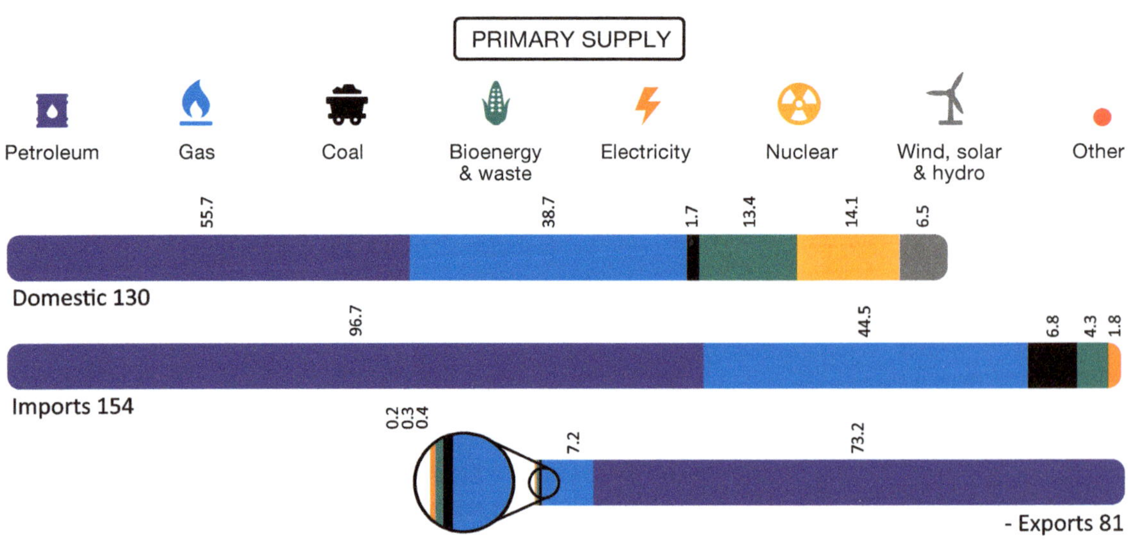

Source: © OGUK's Energy Transition Outlook 2019

Photo 1. Industrial landscape, Seal Sands

Source: © Brian Matthews, published with permission

2.1 Generation capacity and interconnectors

In 2019 the UK's generation mix tipped in favour of low-carbon forms of generation over conventional fossil fuels. The combined low-carbon share (low carbon is typically taken to refer to nuclear and renewables) is currently around 53%, but it is rising each year. In fact, the rise over the last couple of years would have been more significant if the growth in renewables had not been tempered by a fall in nuclear generation (attributable to a bad run of unforeseen outages and maintenance work). In terms of overall technology types, natural gas is the main fuel for electricity generation in the UK, accounting for around 40% of the mix (although now falling slightly). Together with the much more carbon-intensive coal- and oil-fuelled forms of power, the fossil generation share has now fallen for the first time to less than half. The full capacity breakdown is currently approximately as follows: natural gas 30%, nuclear 9%, renewables 43%, coal/oil/open cycle gas turbine (OCGT) 17% and pumped storage 2.5% (rounded to the nearest %).

Imports over interconnectors account for around 5% of total supply (trending upwards as more interconnectors are built and there is more short-term fluctuation in the UK generation mix). The purpose of interconnectors is to provide cross-border transmission capacity that connects different electricity markets, which means operators can respond to price differences across markets (eg, those driven by localised weather patterns). The UK currently has around 5GW of subsea cable interconnector capacity. These are with France (the 2GW IFA), the Netherlands (the 1GW BritNed), Northern Ireland (the 500MW Moyle), the Republic of Ireland (the 500MW East West) and, most recently, Belgium (the 1GW Nemo). It also has a pipeline of approximately 11GW of projects proposed or under construction by 2025. This includes the 1.4GW Viking Link, which will connect Britain and Denmark and, at 472 miles once completed in 2023, will be the longest interconnector in the world.

It is worth noting that the installed capacity share for renewables will increase at a faster rate than their share of the electricity generation mix. This is because wind and solar can only generate in favourable weather conditions, so there will be longer periods when they are not operating at peak output. Nonetheless, the UK now has around 108GW of installed electricity generation capacity, which has generally trended upwards in a linear fashion from 1996 (with some downward blips attributable to large coal and nuclear plant closures). Over the same period, total electricity generated peaked in 2005, having risen steadily since 1996 (meaning that in 2018 electricity generation was at its lowest level since 1996). This was driven by falling demand,

Figure 11: Electricity capacity, 1996 to 2018

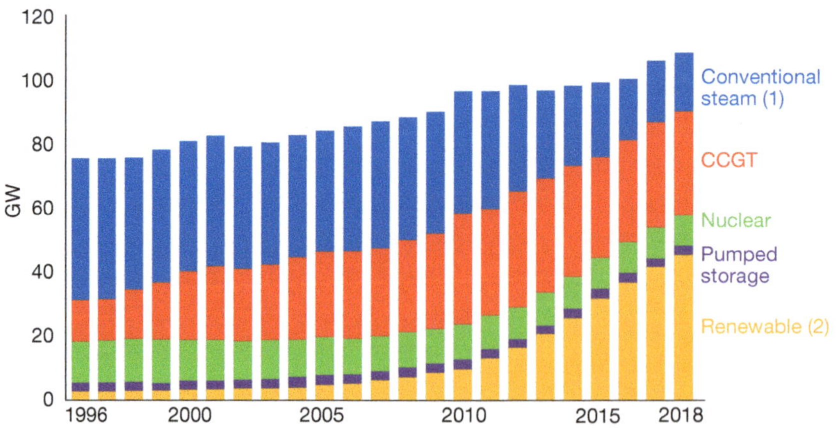

(1) Includes coal, non-CCGT gas, oil and mixed/dual fired. Does not include thermal renewables.
(2) Renewable capacity is on an installed capacity basis. Data for other fuels/technologies relares to Declared Net Capacity from 1996 to 2005, data for 2006 onwards is transmission capacity (TEC).

	1996	2000	2005	2010	2017	GW 2018
Conventional Steam	43.0	39.7	37.1	37.1	18.0	18.0
CCGT	12.7	21.1	25.9	34.0	32.9	31.7
Nuclear	12.9	12.5	11.9	10.9	9.4	9.3
Pumped Storage	2.8	2.8	2.8	2.7	2.7	2.7
Renewable	2.3	3.0	4.5	9.3	40.3	44.3
Total	**73.6**	**79.0**	**82.1**	**94.0**	**103.3**	**106.1**

Source: © UK Energy in Brief 2019, BEIS (figures taken from the 2019 edition of the "Digest of UK Energy Statistics", published 25 July 2019)

principally due to energy efficiency measures and economic changes (including the offshoring of heavy manufacturing and other energy-intensive industries).

Figure 11 shows the dominance of conventional steam generation (coal, open cycle gas, oil and mixed fired power) in 1996. Combined cycle gas turbines (CCGT) and nuclear reactors accounted for the rest of the installed capacity. Fast forward to 2018 and the story changed drastically: conventional steam power more than halved from 43GW to 18GW, CCGTs more than doubled from 13GW to 32GW and renewables came out of nowhere to move from just 2GW to 44GW. That means renewable technologies now account for around 43% of UK installed generating capacity, giving it a larger share than all forms of non-conventional steam generation in 1996. That proportion is growing all the time as larger offshore wind farms commission and large coal (and soon, nuclear) power stations close. As attractive as that sounds from an environmental perspective, the loss of large centralised forms of generation has introduced a number of network management and balancing challenges, which are explored in chapter VIII. It is worth being aware that some reports of installed capacity 'derate' the renewable share to account for its intermittency. The purpose of de-rating is to allow a 'read across' for different technology types to reflect their actual or likely availability (or, put another way, is an attempt to control the influence of weather for wind and solar generation).

In terms of the ~45GW of installed renewables capacity (which is growing every quarter), onshore wind and solar each account for about 30% of that capacity (with onshore slightly ahead), followed by offshore wind (19%), then bioenergy (17%) and hydro (4%). Over the coming years that proportion will start to shift in favour of offshore wind, as the CfD auction facilitates the deployment of a number of very large offshore projects.

2.2 Electricity generated

The story in the UK is in many respects an accelerated microcosm of the global narrative set out in chapter II. In the first two decades of this century, the electricity generation mix has seen a rapid decline in the prominence of coal-fired generation (down to 16.9TWh from 120TWh) and an almost equivalent growth in renewable generation (up to 109.6TWh from just 10.3TWh). Over that same period, there has been a steady decline in oil-fired and nuclear forms of generation, and a reasonably steady contribution from hydro generation.

Figure 12: Electricity generated by fuel type, 2017 and 2018

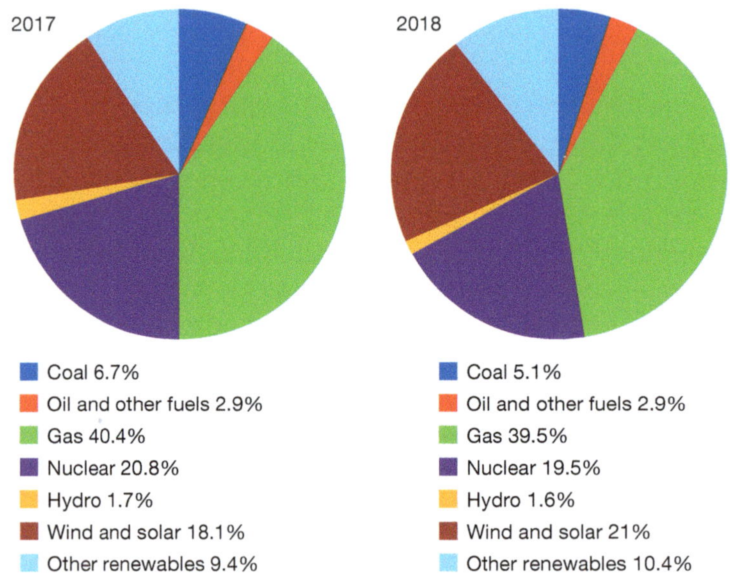

					TWh
	1990	**2000**	**2010**	**2017**	**2018**
Coal	229.8	120.0	107.6	22.5	16.9
Oil & other fuels*	20.7	13.6	10.5	9.8	9.5
Gas	0.4	148.1	175.7	136.7	131.5
Nuclear	63.2	85.1	62.1	70.3	65.1
Hydro	5.6	5.1	3.6	5.9	5.5
Wind & Solar	-	0.9	10.3	61.1	69.8
Other renewables	-	4.3	12.3	31.8	34.8
Total electricity generated	**319.7**	**377.1**	**382.1**	**338.2**	**332.9**

Source: Adapted from UK Energy in Brief 2019, BEIS (figures taken from the 2019 edition of the "Digest of UK Energy Statistics", published 25 July 2019)

Figure 13 below shows the dramatic change in the UK generation mix over the last 30 years, with the decline of once-dominant coal power and the rapid rise of gas and, more recently, renewable generation. As that chart shows, the decline and development of each technology has not followed a smooth path, largely because there is an interdependence between the traditional forms of generation and their underlying market drivers. For example, coal power trended downwards until around 2010 when high winter demand resulted in a dramatic rise in generation, which then continued for a couple of years due to high gas prices. This meant that, for a time, the proportion of electricity generated from coal once again exceeded that of gas. Thereafter, coal plant closures, environmental legislation, strong carbon pricing and the penetration of wind and solar generation has seen coal fall to record lows.

Wind and solar, being fuel-free forms of dispatch, generate independently of the market prices that determine the operating

Figure 13: Electricity supplied by fuel type, 1990 to 2018

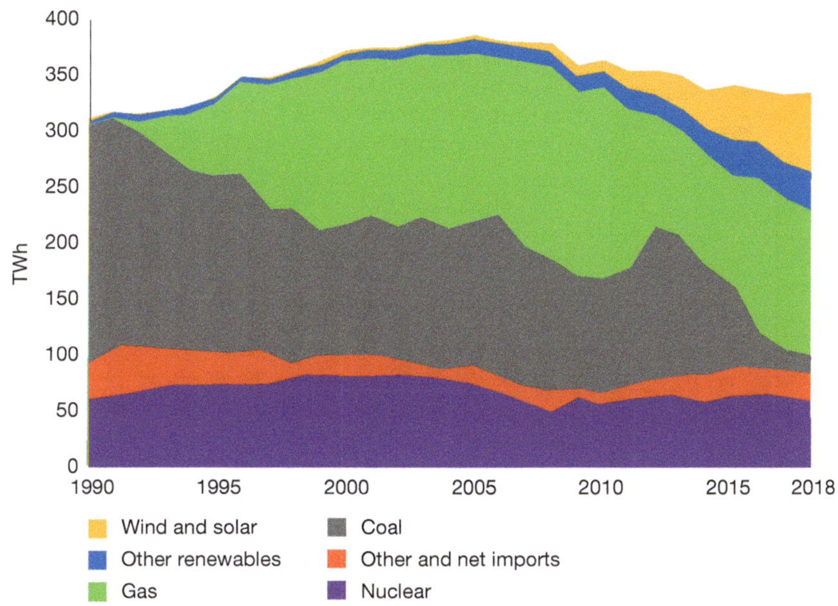

Source: © UK Energy in Brief 2019, BEIS (figures taken from the 2019 edition of the "Digest of UK Energy Statistics", published 25 July 2019)

profile and relative competitiveness of coal and gas. For example, the increase in the carbon floor price from £9/tonne to £18/tonne of CO2 in April 2015 is considered to be the main driver for the shift in generation from coal to gas, meaning coal now only operates during the periods of highest demand. There is a slight irony here in that although wind and solar are not thought of as baseload technologies,[28] they share a certain similarity to baseload in that their generating profile is not really determined by prevailing market prices.

Renewable electricity accounted for a record 33% of electricity generated in the UK during 2018, which is an amazing 3.8% higher than the year before. In 2000, that figure was just 2.6%. The growing dominance of wind (both onshore and offshore) can be seen from Figure 14 below. Although bioenergy (around two thirds of which is wood pellets used in biomass-fired plants) dominates on a 'fuel input' basis, conversion losses in the firing of thermal renewables detract from their 'electricity produced' share (by contrast, non-thermal renewable forms of generation are often considered to be 100% efficient because they do not have conversion losses). The breakdown of the 33% (renewable electricity generated) share is approximately: 32% bioenergy, 28% onshore wind, 24% offshore wind, 12% solar and 5% hydro, showing that unlike the global scene in chapter II, wind technology plays a far more significant role in renewable generation in the UK than solar.

Figure 14: Electricity generation from renewable sources since 2000

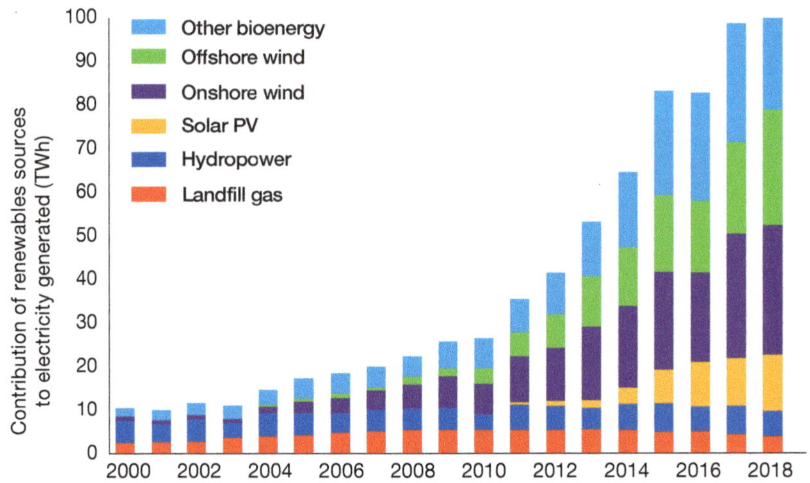

Note: Hydro bar includes shoreline wave/tidal (0.009 TWh in 2018)

	1990	2000	2010	2017	TWh 2018
Onshore wind	–	0.9	7.2	28.7	30.2
Offshore wind	–	–	3.1	20.9	26.7
Solar PV	–	–	0.0	11.5	12.9
Hydro	5.2	5.1	3.6	5.9	5.5
Landfill Gas	0.1	2.2	5.2	4.3	3.9
Other Bioenergy	0.5	1.7	7.0	27.5	30.8
Total Renewables	**5.8**	**9.9**	**26.2**	**98.8**	**110.0**

Source: © UK Energy in Brief 2019, BEIS (figures taken from the 2019 edition of the "Digest of UK Energy Statistics", published 25 July 2019)

3. The relationship between capacity and electricity generated in the UK

The ratio of the amount of electricity actually generated as a proportion of a technology's installed capacity is referred to as its load factor. The load factor is a useful explanation of the utilisation of a form of generation. It serves as a reminder that technologies with the highest installed capacities do not necessarily contribute the largest share of generation. Unfortunately, renewables' load factors are particularly influenced by weather, hence the UK has relatively unfavourable climatic conditions for solar (which is dependent on the number and intensity of sunlight hours) and, accordingly, solar's load factor is only around 11%. This low load factor explains why solar can account for 30% of renewable generation capacity but only 12% of renewable's share of electricity generated. Onshore wind fares a little better at 26% and offshore wind better still at 40–50% (as offshore turbines are larger and have access to higher and more regular wind speeds). Bioenergy, being a 'fuelled' form of generation, has a much higher load factor of around 58%, which explains how biomass can have only the fourth-lowest share of installed capacity for renewable technology but the highest share of generation.

IV. UK policy and the road to Net Zero

1. UK energy policy

Chapters II and III set the scene globally and domestically for progress on decarbonising electricity supply. This chapter focuses much more specifically on UK energy policy, centring principally on the new Net Zero ambition, which has redefined the conversation on how energy consumption will change over the next 30 years.

2019 was a watershed year for UK energy policy. The first seven years of the last decade saw a steady stream of renewable energy projects commission, but thereafter renewables took a heavy hit from the withdrawal of public subsidy mechanisms. The withdrawal of the FiT, the closure of the RO scheme to onshore wind and solar, and the limitation of technologies in the second and third allocation rounds of the CfD auction all caused renewable project development activity to tank in 2018, and then only stutter forward into the new decade.

In fact, of the major 'green' technologies, only offshore wind continued to see strong sector growth as the CfD regime went from (modest) strength to strength. But the mood music started to change in the summer of 2019 when Net Zero became law (actual law, not just policy). With very little in the way of prior public debate, the government legally obliged itself to ensure that by 2050, GHGEs were effectively eliminated.[29] This is a remarkable commitment; the UK was the first major economy to do it. Perhaps unsurprisingly given the nature of the challenge and the level of political upheaval over 2019, it is taking some time for credible proposals to come forward on how the government intends to deliver on its promise. This was shown rather publicly in the much-delayed 2019 Energy White Paper, which became one of the many policy casualties at the altar of the Brexit basilisk.

This chapter explains what Net Zero is, how it came about and what it might take to deliver it. It also looks at related policy that is ancillary to securing Net Zero, including the UK's policies on renewable technology support.

2. Policy development – overview

This section presents a high-level description of the development of UK energy policy, and serves to set the context for the emergence of Net Zero in 2019.

2.1 Climate Change Act 2008

The Climate Change Act of 2008 introduced legally binding GHGE reduction targets on the UK government and established the Committee on Climate Change (CCC). It introduced a target of an 80% reduction in GHGEs from the 1990 baseline by 2050.

2.2 Coalition government 2011 budget

The 2011 coalition government's budget established the Carbon Price Floor (CPF) from 2013 as a top-up to the EU Emissions Trading Scheme (EU ETS). The purpose of the CPF was to ensure carbon-emitting forms of generation paid a tariff for their environmentally damaging emissions. It was structured as a tax on the supply of fossil fuels to generators (with the fuels being taxed on their average carbon content). The CPF is discussed in more detail in chapter V.

2.3 Electricity Market Reform (EMR) under the Energy Act 2013

EMR has become the cornerstone of UK electricity policy. Various important decarbonisation initiatives sit under EMR, including carbon price support and the emissions performance standard (which effectively ruled out the development of new unabated coal plants), but probably the two most important developments were the introduction of the following:

- **Capacity Market (CM):** The CM provides regular payments on a kilowatt (kW) per year basis (referred to as CM payments) to reliable forms of capacity in return for that capacity being available during times of system stress. The emphasis of the CM is on generation capacity being available if required, not regularly generating per se. Capacity is procured through

"The Climate Change Act of 2008 introduced legally binding GHGE reduction targets on the UK government and established the Committee on Climate Change (CCC). It introduced a target of an 80% reduction in GHGEs from the 1990 baseline by 2050."

capacity auctions on a rolling four-year-ahead and year-ahead (of delivery year) programme and is open on a technology-neutral basis to generators, storage projects and demand side response (DSR) participants. In either case, capacity providers are paid to be able to provide electricity or reduce demand when required. Conversely, penalties are imposed if capacity providers fail to meet their commitments during a system stress event. The CM is discussed in more detail in chapter VI.

- **Contracts for Difference (CfD):** The CfD regime provides long-term price stability to renewable and low-carbon forms of generation, facilitating a lower cost of capital and a more economically efficient final cost to consumers. The primary advantage to CfD generators is reduced exposure to volatile wholesale electricity prices. They still sell energy into the market as usual (eg, through a Power Purchase Agreement), but a pre-agreed 'strike price' in the CfD contract removes their exposure to fluctuating electricity prices. When the wholesale price exceeds the strike price, the generator is required to pay back the difference, which ensures end consumers (who pay for the costs of the CfD in their energy bills) are protected from excessive overpayments to generators. The CfD is also discussed in more detail in chapter VI.

- **Levy Control Framework (LCF):** The LCF has now been replaced by the Control for Low Carbon Levies (CfLCL). The CfLCL introduced a budget to cover all renewable tariffs, effectively capping payments under the RO, FiT and other low-carbon subsidy schemes, in recognition that the widespread uptake of RO etc backed schemes had far exceeded the Department of Energy and Climate Change's (as it then was) expectations.

2.4 The Renewables Obligation (RO)

The RO is a policy introduced by the UK government to support the development of renewable generation technology. It forms one of a number of low-carbon policy mechanisms that were intended to help discharge the UK's obligations under the Renewable Energy Directive 2009 (RED I).[30] The RO obliges all licensed electricity suppliers to source a certain proportion of their electricity supply from renewable sources. Renewables Obligation Certificates (ROCs) are issued by Ofgem to generators and prove that electricity has been generated from accredited renewable sources (as opposed to conventional power sources). Generators may then sell their ROCs to suppliers, so that the suppliers can submit them to Ofgem to satisfy their RO accounts. Although it has its policy roots in RED I, the financial rationale of the RO was to help subsidise the higher cost of renewable generation. This was intended to mitigate its competitive disadvantage against cheaper conventional forms of power (coal- and gas-fired generation) or rival low-carbon generation (nuclear) and so encourage private sector investment. In this sense, the RO is complementary to policies that specifically make generating electricity through carbon-intensive sources more expensive, namely the EU ETS and the UK CPF.

When a supplier is unable to submit a sufficient number of ROCs to satisfy its obligations in respect of an obligation period, it must instead pay a buy-out price. Where suppliers are unable to submit ROCs or pay the buy-out price (generally because of insolvency – of new entrants have already exited the supply market), a system of mutualisation exists whereby all other suppliers are required to make good the shortfall. The RO forms one of a number of schemes and policies introduced by the UK government to support renewable generation. Although the RO closed to new projects in 2017, projects that were accredited before the cut-off date will continue to receive ROCs until the earlier of the expiry of their 20-year term or the RO scheme finally closing in 2037.

The RO scheme has two characteristics that ensured it has been successful in delivering its policy objectives. They are, first, a means of guaranteeing the distinction between electricity produced from renewable and conventional sources and, second, an unambiguous means of allowing suppliers to demonstrate their compliance with their allocated targets. Fundamental to the success of the regime is that certificates are limited in supply, are easily transferable and are indirectly linked to a financial reference price (the penalty for failing to satisfy the obligation, referred to as the buy-out price).

For projects accredited before the RO scheme closed, revenue from ROCs is an incredibly valuable part of the project's revenue stream. In fact, the significant drop-off in renewable project development in 2018 (particularly onshore wind) has been attributed to the closure of the RO scheme and the loss of the associated ROC revenue. In the absence of ROC revenue, new build projects that are not eligible for the CfD have to find and negotiate a power purchase agreement (PPA) as a route to market or rely on merchant power prices, although more recently utilities and trading houses have been willing to fix prices for longer periods (eg, up to seven years). The difficulties this presents for projects is discussed in further detail in chapter VI.

2.5 The Feed-in Tariff (FiT)

The FiT was introduced in 2010 to provide generators of smaller projects (less than 5MW) with a predictable revenue stream over a 20–25-year period. There are two elements to the FiT: a generation tariff (for producing power) and a fixed export tariff (being the price of the power produced), both indexed to the retail price index (RPI). The generation tariff is analogous to the receipt by a generator of payments for ROCs (whereas the export tariff is the price it is paid for its electricity). To avoid double recovery (and unfairly burdening customers), a project cannot participate in both the RO and FiT schemes. FiT payments are made by suppliers based on their market share of total electricity supply (irrespective of whether they could source electricity cheaper on the wholesale market). The early closure of the FiT scheme was forecast in the autumn 2017 budget (when the CfLCL replaced the LCF) and the government subsequently announced, after a remarkably fast consultation, the scheme's closure in March 2019. This announcement led to a rush of projects seeking to accredit under the FiT scheme before it closed, as low wholesale market prices at the time meant that most FiT generators could achieve better value through accessing the export tariff (even if that meant forgoing favourable embedded benefits).

2.6 Smart Export Guarantee (SEG)

The FiT regime has now been replaced with the Smart Export Guarantee (SEG), partly due to a sharp drop in the installation of commercial and residential solar projects following the FiT's closure. The SEG scheme commenced on 1 January 2020 and is intended to enable anaerobic digestion, hydro projects, small combined heat and power (CHP) plants (of less than 50 kW), and onshore wind and solar projects of up to 5MW to receive payments for their exported electricity. Crucially though, the SEG scheme does not provide the same tariff certainty for generators and many in the industry are concerned that this lack of revenue certainty will prevent smaller projects from getting off the ground. This is because, unlike the FiT, the SEG does not have a mandated minimum tariff. A supplier must simply provide a tariff that is greater than zero at all times of export. Beyond that, electricity suppliers are free to determine the nature of the tariff they offer to small generators (provided they otherwise meet the requirements of the FiT scheme). Although it is still early days for the SEG scheme, several suppliers (although by no means a majority) have offered what is considered to be a fair tariff.

3. The emergence of Net Zero

The term Net Zero entered energy industry parlance in 2019 and is now routinely used as a proxy for the elevated carbon-neutral agenda. It specifically refers to the legally binding requirement for the UK to procure that its total GHGEs in 2050 are reduced by 100% of the equivalent levels in 1990. What that really means in practice is that total GHGEs must be equal to (or less than) emissions recovered from the environment. Somewhat misleadingly, the debate has become almost entirely about CO2, but there are many GHGs and some

"The term Net Zero entered energy industry parlance in 2019 and is now routinely used as a proxy for the elevated carbon-neutral agenda. It specifically refers to the legally binding requirement for the UK to procure that its total GHGEs in 2050 are reduced by 100% of the equivalent levels in 1990."

(eg, methane) have a much greater warming effect than CO_2 (in equivalent volumes). Now that Net Zero has become law in the UK, the conversation has become about how to deliver it, at what cost and by when. How, though, did Net Zero come about?

- The Climate Change Act 2008 introduced a legal commitment on the UK government to reduce long-term GHGEs by 80% of 1990 levels by 2050. The Act refers to the "net UK carbon account for the year [being] at least 80% lower than the 1990 baseline". Section 2 of the Act gave the Secretary of State (of Business, Energy and Industrial Strategy (BEIS)) the power to amend the target, either through the percentage or the baseline year, if there have been "significant developments in ... scientific knowledge about [climate change] or ... in law or policy". The Act also established the CCC, whose purpose is to advise the UK government on emissions targets and to report to Parliament on progress made in reducing GHGEs and preparing for climate change.
- Outside the UK, the global Paris Agreement was signed in September 2015 and became effective in November 2016. It contained a commitment to peak global GHGEs as soon as possible and to hold the increase in the global average temperature to "well below 2°C above pre-industrial levels" while also pursuing efforts to limit the temperature increase to 1.5°C. It required the individual member states to determine their own domestic GHGE reduction targets referred to as their respective NDCs. These NDCs provide a mechanism for tracking collective progress in delivering the ambition of the Paris Agreement.
- Following the Paris Agreement, the IPCC were invited to deliver a report on the impact of global warming above the 1.5°C level and the associated reduction in GHGEs required to limit the rise in global temperatures to 1.5°C. The IPCC's October 2018 report advised that limiting global warming to 1.5°C was possible but would require unprecedented "rapid and far reaching" changes in all aspects of society, with a need to reach Net Zero by 2050. The report, very worryingly, noted that global warming is likely to increase by 3°C above pre-industrial levels by 2100. It is easy to be flippant about apparently small-sounding temperature variations, but the reality is that a lot of environmental studies have shown that even very small variations (measured in tenths of a degree) have demonstrable, and often irreversible, physical and ecological impacts.
- As a result of the IPCC's 2018 report, Claire Perry MP (then Minister for Energy and Clean Growth) asked the CCC on 15 October 2018 for updated advice on the UK's existing GHGEs reduction level and target date. Responding to that request, the

CCC published its Net Zero report on 2 May 2019. The CCC recommended the UK set a target of Net Zero GHGEs by 2050. Interestingly (in light of subsequent commitments by political parties and pressure groups), it did not consider it credible to reach Net Zero earlier. The CCC's recommendations were wide-ranging and included the following: a split-UK target (Scotland by 2045, England by 2050 and Wales by 2055); the inclusion of international aviation and shipping emissions; the exclusion of international carbon credits (as a form of offsetting); and the rather damning observation that "current policy is insufficient for even the existing targets". Notwithstanding its views on policy, the CCC concluded that achieving Net Zero was achievable with known technologies (although this arguably overlooks the lack of a successful track record for several of those technologies), alongside major changes in people's behaviour. The latter point is often overlooked in the debate that followed the report.

- The CCC emphasised the importance of clear policy focus across all key sectors, including: power generation (where it foresaw a need to quadruple the supply of green electricity); heating (where drastic improvements are required in energy efficiency, insulation and low-carbon heating); large-scale CCUS; agriculture practice changes (large volumes of methane are produced by ruminants); the treatment of waste (with a target of sending no biodegradable waste to landfill after 2025); research and development (R&D) in hydrogen as a fuel source; and, perhaps most importantly, fundamental changes in consumer behaviour. The latter includes significantly lower consumption of meat and dairy, and the earlier adoption of EVs by 2035.
- The CCC suggested the cost of meeting the Net Zero target was still within the existing cost range for the 80% target, being 1–2% of GDP. This is largely attributable to cost savings in key technologies. There is some debate about the actual cost projections, and that will obviously continue for so long as the means required to deliver Net Zero remain uncertain, but a common objection will be that the costs of inaction far outweigh the costs of prevention and mitigation. It is also important to consider the value of other benefits captured (primarily in terms of health and environmental impact). As the energy economist Dieter Helm noted at the time though, it is very hard to usefully predict cost as a percentage of GDP over these timeframes.
- BEIS accepted the headline recommendation and introduced secondary legislation on 12 June 2019 to require Net Zero GHGEs by 2050, by amending the Climate Change Act (replacing 80% with 100%). It did not adopt the CCC's suggestion of accelerating the deadline in Scotland (on account of its more

favourable geography), nor the exclusion of international carbon credits. It has also introduced a five-year review to ensure the UK is not left at a competitive disadvantage if other economies do not follow the same policy. That draft legislation became law, and has had the interesting effect of inspiring individual regions, cities, airports and companies to announce their own ambitions of carbon neutrality in much earlier timescales (2030 being a favourite).

- Following the Net Zero report, the CCC then published its 2019 Progress Report. This was closely followed by National Grid's Future Energy Scenarios 2019 (FES 19), which featured a rather rushed analysis of the additional considerations it would take to reach Net Zero (National Grid's four original scenarios are based on the unamended 80% target). What follows is a summary of the conclusions in, first, the CCC's 2019 Progress Report and, second, National Grid's FES 2019.

4. The Committee on Climate Change's 2019 Progress Report

One of the CCC's main roles is to monitor progress in reducing emissions and achieving carbon budgets and targets. It does this by producing annual Progress Reports to Parliament, which provide an update on the government's progress towards meeting climate

"Given how readily the Net Zero recommendation was accepted by the government, the CCC's 2019 Progress Report might have been expected to take a reasonably conciliatory approach. That hope quickly evaporated as the CCC lined up an iron punch in a velvet glove."

targets. Given how readily the Net Zero recommendation was accepted by the government, the CCC's 2019 Progress Report might have been expected to take a reasonably conciliatory approach. That hope quickly evaporated as the CCC lined up an iron punch in a velvet glove. Opening its report with the velveteen, "We welcome strongly the UK Parliament's decision to make net zero law", the CCC followed with the more ferrous observation that "there is only limited evidence of the present government taking it seriously". By the end of 2019, it was not clear that the government had done any more to give the CCC comfort. A change of personnel at BEIS and a rather desultory hodgepodge of regurgitated funding announcements leading into the Conservative's autumn party conference did little to suggest there was a strong policy plan to deliver Net Zero. The Conservative Manifesto for the December 2019 general election only saw a mildly upgraded offshore wind ambition rather than a wholesale re-imagining of energy policy along the lines of that proposed by some of the other parties.

The CCC drew attention to the government's failure to deliver all but one of its 2018 headline policy actions, the failure even to partially progress ten of those actions, the fact that only seven of 24 progress indicators are on track (down to only two if the power sector is discounted), the significant divergence in the fourth and fifth carbon budgets and a wider policy gap on emissions generally. Transport, buildings, agriculture and land use were all identified as having shown insufficient progress.

Despite some faint praise for BEIS in having made "good progress in the power sector", it was subsequently chastised for being too slow in incentivising the development of CCUS, not investing in heat pump and low-carbon hydrogen technology and for holding back the deployment of onshore wind. The CCC also noted that BEIS needed to do more to provide a route to market for onshore wind and solar generation. Government activity was deemed to be "well short of [that] required for the net-zero target". The Net Zero journey for the government had not got off to the smoothest of starts.

5. Future energy scenarios 2019: Net Zero aspects

National Grid's Future Energy Scenarios (published in July 2019) (FES 19) cannot be criticised for the scale of its ambition in outlining the steps required to deliver Net Zero. Despite the new Net Zero target only becoming law late in its publication lifecycle, FES 19 was able to conclude that Net Zero "is achievable [but] requires immediate action across all key technologies and policy areas". As mentioned earlier in this chapter in section 3, FES 19 was prepared with the existing 80% reduction target in mind, so the bolt-on 'sensitivity analysis' had to focus on the additional steps to close the final, and inevitably most intransigent, 20% of emission reductions.

FES 19 articulates the central challenge of Net Zero extremely well: "the 80% decarbonisation target can be reached through multiple technology pathways, but Net Zero requires greater action across all solutions" and "at a significantly greater scale than assumed in any of [the] core scenarios". It is often assumed that Net Zero is a government problem, to be solved with appropriate policy intervention and investment support. As touched on in section 3, that is simply not the case, and FES 19 draws attention to the dual requirement of both "coordinated policy changes" (macro level) and "significant behaviour change" (micro level). Interestingly, although the discussion has now become binary (a 100% reduction is an 'all or nothing' outcome), it is easily forgotten that FES 19's Net Zero 'sensitivity analysis' only gets to 96% emission reductions. The report concluded that to get to 100% would require the development of new "commercially unproven technologies", which is certainly possible over the next 30 years, but also a potential vulnerability for the Net Zero obligation. It is important to remember that the purpose of the FES 19 analysis was to show what it might take to deliver the Net Zero ambition from a system operator's perspective; it was not intended as a formula for government policy on how that should actually be delivered.

These are the key messages for each sector from the Net Zero aspect of FES 19:

5.1 Heating homes

Around 18% of the UK's CO_2 emissions come from the residential sector (mostly heating and cooking).[31] Decarbonising heating is therefore very important from an emissions reduction perspective. In the Net Zero sensitivity analysis, it is anticipated that homes will need at least 36% less energy for heating than today (due to efficiencies they will have achieved). Also, all that heating will need to come through green power sources. To achieve this turnaround the following will be required:

- significant improvements in thermal efficiencies of homes (85% of homes need to be "very thermally efficient", at least EPC class C, by 2050);
- continued improvements in appliance efficiency;
- immediate and large-scale rollout of heat pumps (2.5m by 2030); and
- the provision of heat through electric or hybrid heat pumps using zero-carbon electricity and/or decarbonised gas (being either biogas from anaerobic digestion or green hydrogen).

Introducing thermal efficiency sounds simple but consider the age of UK residential property, and the difficulties and costs associated with retrofitting insulation (consider also even the challenges associated with rolling out smart meters). To make matters worse, the BEIS Commons Select Committee subsequently criticised the government's "failing energy efficiency policy", noting in its July 2019 review that the government was "off track to meet its Clean Growth Strategy targets; major policy gaps still exist".

5.2 Growth in generation capacity

National Grid's existing Two Degrees scenario was already very ambitious in terms of how much additional generation capacity it required to deliver the 80% reduction in GHGEs. Net Zero raises the stakes even further. Total installed generation capacity in the UK is currently 108GW, and FES 19 predicts the need for this to more than double to around 263GW by 2050, if Net Zero is to be secured. This massive increase in capacity assumes a six-fold increase in offshore wind generation (from 2018 levels) and the largescale deployment of small modular reactors (a form of power generation that is not even proven at a commercial level). See Figure 15.

On top of that, almost all the existing generation fleet will need to be replaced or repowered, as much of it will have reached the end of its economic generating life by 2050. Peak electricity demand is anticipated to rise to approximately double today's levels. These are

Figure 15: Installed electricity generation capacity (the important comparison is 2018 compared to the new Net Zero sensitivity)

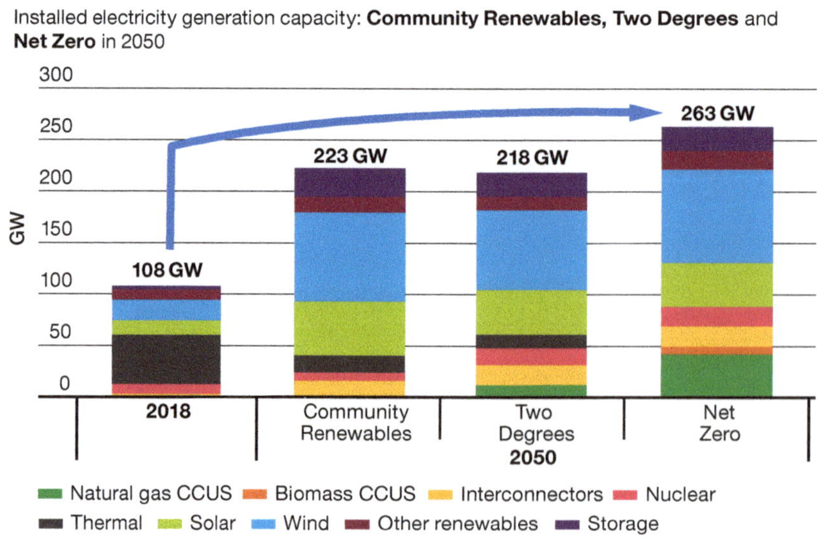

Source: Adapted from © National Grid's Future Energy Scenario (July 2019)

hugely ambitious targets, and current policy has not helped by creating an extremely tight bottleneck in renewable project developments (for example, onshore wind development fell by 80% in 2018 to the lowest level of new installations since 2011). In the clamour to sign up to Net Zero, it has been disappointingly easy to overlook quite how fundamental the scale of the challenge is.

5.3 Net Zero actually means negative zero – sequestration

FES 19 acknowledged that not all GHG-emitting processes can be entirely eliminated, so other sectors will have to get to zero and beyond to ensure the overall emission level is balanced at zero. This means existing GHGEs need to be removed from the atmosphere to offset the continuation of emissions from these activities. That is a considerable challenge: National Grid anticipates that 37m tonnes of CO2 will need to be removed from the atmosphere using techniques such as biomass power generation paired with CCS (referred to as bioenergy carbon capture storage (BECCS)) and nature-based sequestration processes, such as reforestation and rewilding. One tonne of CO2 has a volume of around 500 m3, which is about the size of a hot air balloon, and stays in the atmosphere for around 100 years, so this is far from straightforward. The BECCS approach uses plant-based fuels (biofuels, eg, wood pellets) that have captured CO2 from the atmosphere during their growth and then recaptures the CO2 produced in their combustion to prevent it reentering the atmosphere. Over several cycles, this process would, in principle, bring down the level of CO2 currently in the atmosphere.

5.4 Indispensability of carbon capture, use and storage (CCUS) technology

BECCS (as a possible source of negative emissions) is the solution to addressing those areas where carbon reduction is very difficult. However, even National Grid's Two Degrees scenario leans heavily on CCUS as the answer to the continued reliance on natural gas, which would otherwise continue to emit GHGEs. Natural gas, currently responsible for around 40% of UK power generation, does not get phased out of the scenario entirely but becomes rebranded as 'natural gas CCUS'. Gas itself is still absolutely essential in the energy system: for the production of hydrogen (through steam methane reforming); for industry (for heating processes); and for electricity generation (to supplement increased renewable generation and the phase out of coal and nuclear). Again, the reliance on CCUS represents a significant vulnerability in the Net Zero ambition as there are only very early stage pilot projects operating in the UK, and experience globally is also limited. Some of these issues are discussed in further detail in chapter VII.

5.5 Electric vehicles (EVs)

The existing 80% target already anticipated the widescale take up of EVs (NG estimate around 35m), and the CCC subsequently made clear that the ban on non-electric cars needed to be brought forward significantly, from 2040 to 2030. National Grid recognised that this required no (as opposed to a few) conventional or hybrid vehicles to be on the road in 2050. Moreover, the network of batteries within EVs will potentially open up a means of providing grid flexibility and so help integrate a higher level of renewable generation on the system. This assumes that over 75% of EVs will use 'smart charging' technology by 2050 (smart charging and 'vehicle to grid' services will be key to the success of the transition to EVs). The premise of smart charging is that vehicle batteries will charge when prices are low and, in principle, will be able to export to the system during times of stress (low supply and high demand). This is a good example of the required combination of technological and behavioural change to deliver Net Zero. It is also reflective of the significant digitisation of low-carbon infrastructure. National Grid anticipates a staggering 2.8 trillion data points will be collected in 2050 to understand EV charging patterns alone. The Net Zero sensitivity also assumes heavy goods vehicles (HGVs) will use hydrogen as a fuel, meaning more demand on hydrogen production through electrolysis or natural gas with CCS (ie, through steam methane reforming).

"Net Zero will not be secured with policy and technology alone. Although climate change awareness is increasing, it is not happening at the pace required. Net Zero is as much as anything a battle for hearts and minds."

5.6 Interoperability

National Grid recognised the need for far more interaction between the gas and electricity markets, as they come together in new applications. For example, domestic and industrial hybrid heat pumps will use a mix of hydrogen gas and electricity, depending on ambient temperatures (so that gas is only used if an energy 'boost' is required when temperatures are low). There are also significant changes required within the systems, as electricity generation needs to become entirely low carbon, rather than the 53% low carbon it is today. There is also a fundamental move way from transmission connected generation (currently at 71%) in favour of decentralised generation. As mentioned in section 5.4 above, natural gas will either need to become carbon neutral (through CCUS) or be replaced by hydrogen. This is why FES 19 emphasises the importance of a 'whole system' approach to energy, with the attendant need to promote new ways of designing and operating those systems.

5.7 Behavioural

National Grid recognised that Net Zero will not be secured with policy and technology alone. Its Net Zero sensitivity assumes consumers are "highly engaged in energy matters, and buy only very efficient appliances" and "use smart appliances to shift their electricity demand". This is all laudable, but cynics may be concerned about the success of previous attempts to instigate wide-ranging behavioural changes. For example, the smart meter roll-out has experienced many difficulties and, although climate change awareness is increasing, it is not happening at the pace required. This echoes the CCC's observation that "over half of the emission cuts to reach net-zero emissions require people to do things differently. The public must be engaged in the challenge". Net Zero is as much as anything a battle for hearts and minds.

6. Delivering Net Zero

As things stand, there is an inherent conflict in many of the policies, or at least a worrying dissonance between long-term aspirations and short-term realities. For example, compare these things:

- the absolute indispensability of BECCs and CCUS under Net Zero with government policy to date on CCUS (eg, the cancelled 2015 CCS demonstration programme) and the nascent state of the associated CO2 capture and storage technology;
- the importance of new build nuclear power with both the start-stop competition in the last five years to get small modular reactors (SMRs) off the ground (and again, the early development stage and long regulatory process associated with licensing nuclear technology), and the limited progress and higher cost of developing a new fleet of nuclear power

stations compared with that envisaged in the government's 2011 National Policy Statement on nuclear power;

- the aspirations for hydrogen as a carbon-free substitute for natural gas with the fact that its production globally currently accounts for more GHGEs than the economies of the UK and Indonesia combined;
- the importance of developing electrolysis for hydrogen production (as an application of the oversupply of renewable capacity or where generation is in grid-constrained areas) with the fact that only around 0.1% of hydrogen globally is produced this way; and
- the massive generation capacity gap identified by the CCC and National Grid with the government's policy on supporting renewable projects (as shown in its reluctance to increase the third round 2019 CfD 6GW capacity cap or to revisit its policy on supporting onshore wind and solar).

Looking at these points alone, it is hard to be confident that the policy ambition and the willingness to deliver it sit comfortably together. This appears to be compounded by the new Conservative government's somewhat lukewarm statements on climate change and energy policy in the aftermath of the December 2019 general election. Some of the particular technologies required to support the delivery of Net Zero are explored in greater detail in chapter VII.

V. Generation technologies: going from black to grey

1. Overview

The purpose of this chapter is to give an overview of the main forms of 'traditional' power generation in the UK: coal, nuclear and natural gas. Partly, the aim is to provide context for the development of the new renewable power sector (see chapter VI) but it also helps to frame the policy narrative that has, over time, nudged investment away from large, centrally connected generation to carbon-free, distributed renewable technologies. That transition is most starkly demonstrated by the move away from coal-fired power generation. Natural gas is certainly not low carbon, but it is far less carbon intensive than coal-fired generation and fulfils a very valuable role in the energy mix in supporting the transition to a greater renewable power base. Natural gas is highly likely to continue to play a role in the future, particularly when twinned with CCUS technology. Nuclear is a reliable, low-carbon, baseload provider of electricity and has a key role in providing firm capacity in the future, particularly in underpinning grid stability in the context of higher levels of variable (intermittent) renewable forms of generation. That is likely to take the form of a modest number of large, centrally connected units (like the 3.2GW Hinkley Point C in Somerset) and potentially smaller, distributed small modular reactors (see chapter VII).

2. Coal-fired generation

2.1 Summary

The golden age of coal-fired power generation is now well past, but coal was, and in many countries remains, a ubiquitous and cheap form of fuel. As identified in chapter II, the global proliferation of the coal power sector is a major contributor to the continuing rise in GHGEs. In the UK, the widespread development of coal plants in the 1950s and 1960s tracked the prosperity of the UK coal mines. Until very recently, the UK had continuously burned coal for power generation since the opening of Holborn Viaduct power station in 1882. However, a tipping point has now been reached. Solar power produced more electricity than coal for the first time in 2016. In 2018, the UK had its first 24-hour period without any coal generation since 1882 and, in May 2019, the UK ran for 18 days without any (domestic) coal generation (interconnectors are not entirely coal free). That record is unlikely to stand for long as the number of plants that have either closed or announced closure increases. Whereas coal supplied 30% of UK generation as recently as 2014, that figure fell drastically to 5.4% in 2018.

2.2 The coal scene

There are now only six active coal-fired power stations in the UK, which between them have a generating capacity of around 9.5GW. However, two of those plants (RWE's Aberthaw B and SSE's Fiddlers Ferry) closed in early 2020 and the other sites either have plans to close, convert to co-fire biomass or replant to gas (Drax and Eggborough are good conversion examples). In fact, only EDF Energy's West Burton A and Uniper's Ratcliffe have not announced closure or conversion plans (EDF Energy's neighbouring Cottam power station closed in late 2019). Unsurprisingly, since the government's 2015 proclamation that all unabated coal would need to close by 2025, the poor economics of coal power generation has led to a spate of closures and some, more limited, biomass conversions.

2.3 Policy

The combined effect of policies against carbon-based generation and new subsidy regimes to encourage renewables is that coal will not play a role in the UK energy mix beyond 2025. There are three policy developments that caused the decline of coal-fired generation:

(a) Legislation introducing binding restrictions on GHGEs

The main piece of legislation in this category is the Climate Change Act 2008, which introduced the requirement for the UK to reduce GHGEs by 80% of 1990 levels by 2050, now amended to 100% (as described in chapter IV). The Renewable Energy Directives (RED I

Photo 2. West Burton A coal-fired power station, turbine hall

Source: © Brian Matthews, published with permission

and RED II) are also relevant as they introduced a target for the EU to source a proportion of its total energy requirement from renewable sources by 2030.

(b) Legislation prejudicing coal-fired generation

The main policies in this category are, first, power emissions-based legislation, including the Industrial Emissions Directive (IED) and Large Combustion Plant Directive (LCPD), summarised in section 2.4 below; and, second, finance-based legislation, including the EU ETS and CPF:

- The EU ETS is a mandatory 'cap and trade' scheme for GHGs which was introduced in 2005. The scheme sets an EU-wide cap (decreasing over time) on the total amount of permitted GHGEs from energy-intensive sectors, including power stations. Relevant companies are allocated EU Allowances (EUAs), either for free or for a price determined by allowance auctions. Companies are also required to pay a fine for any shortfall of emissions to allowances. As the EU ETS is now in Phase III, power companies are required to purchase their EUAs, rather than receive a free allocation. Surplus allowances are traded on the carbon market via an exchange.
- The CPF is a UK initiative to supplement the EU ETS. The purpose is to introduce a carbon price that encourages low

carbon and renewable generation, which the EU ETS did not achieve on its own. It does this by taxing fossil fuels; requiring fossil fuel generators to pay a carbon price support (CPS) as a top-up to the EU ETS, which gives a carbon floor price target – essentially a total carbon price. There is a tension between the government's desire to maximise the CPS to discourage fossil fuel generation and its desire to not impair the competitiveness of UK businesses against EU competitors, or to excessively increase energy bills for consumers. As such, for the last few years the CPS (which was originally anticipated to rise year on year) has been frozen. As the most carbon-intensive energy source, coal-fired generation has been the technology most affected by the CPF.

Notwithstanding Brexit, the government remains committed to a meaningful carbon price, and it is considering a number of schemes to maintain a total carbon price once the UK leaves the EU ETS, including introducing a parallel regime to the EU ETS scheme.

(c) Subsidies promoting renewables

Three renewable incentives have contributed to the decreasing cost competitiveness of coal: the FiT in 2010, the RO in 2012 and the CfD in 2014. In fact, the only component of the EMR that did not specifically prejudice coal generation, as against other forms of generation, was the CM. Somewhat ironically, CM commitments may have had the perverse effect of keeping the few remaining coal plants on the system into the early 2020s, when it is not otherwise economically efficient for them to stay open. The CM's primary function is to secure sufficient generating capacity to deliver security of supply at times of system stress. As such, coal, existing CCGT and nuclear (as the traditional baseload generators) are the primary benefactors of the CM. Utilities with a mixed generating portfolio had to carefully weigh up their view on these policies. For example, a strong carbon price favours nuclear generation and renewables but is prejudicial to coal- and gas-fired profitability.

2.4 Convert or close

In 2001 the introduction of the LCPD was announced, which would contain emissions limits (for sulphur dioxide and nitrogen oxides) for large carbon emitters. The LCPD became effective in 2008 for plants built before 1987. Plants that were non-compliant with the applicable emissions limits could elect to opt out (although most did invest in flue gas desulphurisation and related technology to allow continued operation), following which they could operate for up to 20,000 hours before 2015, when they were required to close. The LCPD was followed by the Industrial Emissions Directive (IED) in 2016, which consolidated several different pieces of environmental legislation and required all European Union member states to reduce the impact of industrial emissions on the environment.

2.5 Biomass conversion, gas conversion and carbon capture, use and storage (CCUS)

The consequence of the LCPD, IED and government policy generally on coal is that coal plants must close, convert to gas or biomass, or develop CCUS technology. There has been a reasonably limited uptake on both biomass conversion and CCUS development. For biomass, this is largely attributable to the high capital costs of conversion and, to a lesser extent, environmental controversy over the ecological merits of transporting large volumes of wood pellets across the Atlantic. Most plants that elected to convert to biomass have already done so, although some units still plan to convert to gas-fired power. One notable conversion success story is Drax, which announced in November 2019 plans for a threefold increase in its wood pellet production capability by 2027, to support its converted biomass units.

CCUS has a slightly inglorious history, with high-profile investment incentives to develop demonstration technology having been cancelled at late stages, and there has only been a very recent re-emergence of policy support for CCUS. As discussed in chapter IV, the CCC identified in its Net Zero Report that CCUS would play a fundamental part in delivering the 2050 ambition.[32] There have been some high-profile announcements of new CCUS development since the report was published. These include Drax's announcement in February 2019 of the first capture of carbon dioxide in its BECCS pilot and, in May 2019, the Drax, Equinor and National Grid Ventures collaboration agreement to explore how a large-scale CCUS network could be joined with a hydrogen production facility in the Humber region. In late June 2019, Tata Chemicals Europe announced plans to build Britain's first industrial-scale CCUS demonstration plant to trap carbon dioxide from its gas-fired CHP plant, for use in its sodium bicarbonate manufacturing process. CCUS is discussed in further detail in chapter VII.

2.6 Decommissioning

As mentioned in section 2.4 above, some coal plants have chosen the capital-intensive (but long-term survival) route of biomass or gas conversion. Most plants, though, have recognised the challenging policy environment and poor returns from the CM, and announced their closure. In 2019 alone, three coal plants all announced their intention to close, two of them after 50 years of continuous operation.

Demolishing a coal plant is a multi-million-pound, multi-year project that requires significant planning and oversight. The key issues to address include the following:

(a) Contracting strategy (turnkey versus multi-contract)
As with any construction or works project, a careful consideration of the EPC strategy is required at the outset, as this will determine how a number of the other key risks and issues are addressed. Coal plants are suitable for being demolished on both a multi-contract (eg, EPCM) and a single contract/turnkey (EPC) basis. Decommissioning contractors are generally happy to adopt an EPC approach as it gives them full control over the sequence of works. More sophisticated operators who wish to carry out significant parts of the decommissioning programme themselves (eg, preliminary strip-out after going 'cold and dark') may prefer the EPCM approach or a scaled-down EPC scope.

(b) Site risk (including asbestos)
Site risk is an important consideration in any EPC contract, but this is particularly true for coal demolition contracts as sites will generally contain significant quantities of asbestos and other hazardous materials. An owner will generally have access to detailed site records, so might be happy to accept site ground and structure risk, as this will avoid the contractor pricing a premium into the EPC contract. An asbestos survey will be required, and the relationship of the asbestos consultant to the EPC contractor needs careful consideration.

(c) Third-party and nuisance claims
Most sites will have some history of third-party nuisance claims, for example, from noise or ash fallout. The scope for third-party claims has the potential to increase significantly during the demolition phase, when there will be an increased movement of traffic to/from the site as scrap is removed. There will also be a number of controlled explosions to demolish cooling towers and other large structures, which all have the potential to test the patience of an otherwise historically supportive local population.

(d) Scrap strategy
A key value component in the EPC contract will be scrap metal, and there are a number of ways of structuring the valuation and incentivisation approach to scrap. If not thought through fully, the owner is at risk of the contractor obtaining a windfall and also being incentivised to remove the most valuable scrap (eg, copper) first.

(e) End use
While most modern forms of generation will have requirements in their planning consents and leases around decommissioning and reinstatement, coal sites are often built on freehold land and are around 50 years old. Accordingly, the owner may have considerable flexibility in determining how to repurpose the site. The general proposition may be to return to a brownfield site, but bearing in

mind the plant will have valuable TEC (export capacity to the grid), a grid connection and substation, access to water and the full range of utilities, it will also be an attractive site for redevelopment.

3. Nuclear generation

3.1 Overview

The UK has a long and extremely reliable record of generating nuclear power, dating back to the world's first commercial nuclear power station at Calder Hall on the Windscale site (now Sellafield) in 1956. There have since been four programmes of nuclear new build: the first-generation Magnox reactors; the advanced gas-cooled reactor (AGR) programme; the pressurised water reactor (PWR) programme; and nuclear new build today. The Magnox reactors have now all closed (the last, in Anglesey, in 2015), the AGRs and single PWR are still operating (all owned by EDF Energy) and only one new build project is under construction, EDF's Hinkley Point C (HPC) in Somerset.

Nuclear is perhaps the archetypal stable, low-carbon, baseload provider of energy onto the grid, as it has a low marginal cost of generation and very limited ability to offer flexibility. However, the contribution of nuclear is starting to change – nuclear accounted for

"The UK has a long and extremely reliable record of generating nuclear power. However, the contribution of nuclear is starting to change – nuclear accounted for 25% of energy generation in the late 1990s, but that figure hovers around 19% today."

25% of energy generation in the late 1990s, but that figure hovers around 19% today. The declining market share reflects the fact that large volumes of new renewable power have been added to the system, while the output of nuclear has fallen slightly due to challenging availability from the AGRs as they approach the end of their generating life. EDF Energy's seven AGR stations are all expected to close by 2030 and its single PWR, Sizewell B in Suffolk, is expected to close at some point in the 2040s.

3.2 New build nuclear

The Tony Blair government's aspiration of initiating a nuclear renaissance had a pleasant honeymoon, with the establishment of three consortia: Horizon (RWE and Eon), NuGen (Toshiba and GDF Suez) and NNB (EDF Energy). Their combined strategy was to construct more new build capacity than was currently generating, which would have delivered the aspiration of nuclear providing a significant proportion of future energy demand. That aspiration is now looking extremely challenging.

Two things happened that seriously compromised that ambition. The first was the public and industry reaction to Fukushima in 2011, which resulted in Germany turning its back on the nuclear industry and the subsequent withdrawal of German utilities RWE and Eon from the £20 billion Horizon project. The second was (and remains) the failure to design an acceptable nuclear funding model: seen first in Toshiba's inability to sell its £15 billion NuGen project in Cumbria in late 2018 and then in Hitachi's announcement that it was suspending the Horizon project in early 2019.

The Toshiba/NuGen announcement can be read partly in the context of Westinghouse's bankruptcy, but the Hitachi/Horizon announcement has to be seen very much through the lens of the wider reaction to HPC's support package. After extensive negotiations the government offered HPC a 35-year CfD with a CPI-linked strike price of £89.50/MWh if Sizewell C was also built, or £92.50/MWh if it was not. Although this compared favourably with other forms of technology in the first two rounds of the CfD auction, the impact of indexation over the very long tenor of the CfD led to much criticism over the level of public subsidy the project attracted. Accordingly, the government announced it would only offer a much lower CfD for Horizon, up to £75/MWh for the same 35-year term. Even though it had also been willing to take a one-third equity stake in the project and provide the construction debt finance, Hitachi remained concerned about its exposure and eventually walked away from the deal, saying it was too much risk for a private company to carry. At the time of course, construction programmes and budgets on other nuclear projects (such as Flamanville in France and Olkiluoto in Finland) were being significantly and very publicly exceeded.

Photo 3. Hartlepool Nuclear Power Station

Source: © Brian Matthews, published with permission

3.3 Nuclear development costs

The preceding section is a very condensed summary of 10 years of financing challenges to make a simple point: building new build nuclear is incredibly expensive and carries a significant risk profile for privately owned utilities. The government was clear that the finance package given to HPC would not be extended to other new build projects, so a new financing model has to be found to avoid a premature end to the UK's nuclear industry. This puts a lot of pressure on EDF's second development project, Sizewell C in Suffolk, and CGN's plans to develop Bradwell B in Essex.

The success of those projects will rest on finding a solution to a crucial (and in principle controllable) cost component of the strike price: the cost of capital over a prolonged build period. The proportion of the HPC strike price associated with the cost of capital was extremely significant, perhaps as much as half of the project's total cost. Bringing down the LCOE for nuclear requires a new approach to funding.

The government and the nuclear industry now believe the solution lies in a regulated asset base model (RAB) akin to that used in the £4.2 billion Thames Tideway 'super sewer' project. The RAB model aims to de-risk certain elements of the construction phase for private investors by giving them a fixed rate of return (paid for by consumers) over the construction phase. This contrasts with traditional project financed projects, where revenue streams typically do not start to flow until after commissioning. The RAB proposal is discussed in further detail in section 3.6 below.

3.4 Nuclear third-party liability

Those considering contracting with or investing in a nuclear project are inevitably very focused on the (extremely unlikely) possibility of a nuclear incident and the associated liability that might follow. It is worth saying that the reasonably high level of public support in the UK is associated with the extremely rigorous approach to safety by the operator and industry regulator (the Office for Nuclear Regulation). Nonetheless, a key concern for any owner, operator, contractor or investor is the financial and legal consequences of a nuclear incident (of whatever scale). From a legal perspective, nuclear has an unusual liability regime.

Unlike almost any other form of liability, the consequences of a third-party claim arising from a nuclear incident do not align with the normal English law approach of freedom of contract. The UK regime is predicated on the principles of strict and exclusive liability, meaning that except in several narrow cases, the consequences of a third-party claim associated with a nuclear incident are 'channelled' to the licensed operator. The operator cannot contract out of this liability as against a potentially negligent contractor or supplier (save in respect of damage to on-site equipment) but must instead rely on taking out a special insurance policy against the risk of such damage. The reason for strict and exclusive liability on the operator is to encourage wider participation in the industry and to avoid overlapping and therefore inefficient insurance policies.

While this principle applies to most types of possible third-party claim, the extent (in amount) and breadth (in categories of loss) of potential liability, as well as the class of potential claimants, will be significantly extended once certain amendments to the Nuclear Installations Act 1965 (NIA) become effective. These amendments are conditional on the 2004 Protocol to the Paris Convention being ratified by all signatories, which is taking a staggeringly long time to achieve.

The amendments to the NIA are extremely relevant to stakeholders operating in the nuclear industry, as they will increase the statutory protection available to contractors in the event of a nuclear incident. Currently, a contractor may become liable only in certain limited circumstances – the main ones being:

- claims brought in countries not party to the Brussels or Paris Conventions (ie, where the channelling principle does not apply);

- liabilities associated with economic loss and environmental damage; and
- damage to the contractor's own property within the licensed site.

The first category is the most important in the context of the international nuclear supply chain, particularly for US contractors following the Tepco case brought in the US after Fukushima (as the claimants were able to bring a case in the US, even though the event occurred and the damage was sustained in Japan).

Because of concerns with gaps in the third-party liability legislation, contractors generally seek contractual indemnities within their supply agreements or EPC contracts. However, there is an increasing tendency for operators to resist giving them, either by introducing liability caps or refusing to give indemnities at all. It is important to remember that an indemnity can only respond to a claim that is not 'channelled' to the operator in the first place – ie, it must be a liability which falls through one of the statutory gaps. As mentioned above, there are very few such liabilities, so a global indemnity in an EPC contract (in relation to any claim brought following a nuclear incident), while often very hard fought for in negotiations, is often of limited use. When the NIA amendments become effective, that use will become even more limited.

3.5 Brexit and Euratom ('Brexatom')

The concerns of the nuclear industry in relation to Brexit and the associated withdrawal from the Euratom Treaty have now largely been addressed, but it is worth summarising them briefly as they had (and perhaps still have) the potential to significantly interrupt the industry.

The Euratom Treaty (1957) is a cooperation programme to promote the formation and development of Europe's civil nuclear industries. Along with the Treaty on European Union (TEU) and Treaty on the Functioning of the European Union (TFEU), it is the third treaty concerning the European Union. As a matter of law, it was not necessary for the UK to withdraw from the Euratom Treaty when initiating the Article 50 procedure – and almost the entire industry lobbied for Euratom to be carved out of the Brexit process.

It is widely held that the benefits of being in Euratom far outweigh the obligations it imposes (which are largely limited to reporting obligations). In any event, withdrawal simply means having to establish equivalent domestic arrangements to replace the Euratom ones. From the nuclear industry's perspective, the three key concerns of losing Euratom membership were:

(a) Loss of access to the common market

The Euratom community created a common market to trade in nuclear technology and services with the other 27 member states (albeit this was effectively subsumed into the wider EU single market). It also provided the basis for trade with non-EU countries, including the US, Canada and Australia, as Euratom has bilateral agreements with these third countries. The UK is having to enter into new nuclear cooperation agreements (NCAs) with these non-EU countries, generally as a precondition to trade (it is an offence in the US to trade in nuclear material without an NCA in place). Similarly, the UK has to replace its own bilateral NCAs that were predicated on its Euratom membership and it will also need an NCA or more comprehensive trade arrangement with Euratom itself to trade with the remaining EU states.

(b) Safeguards

Reporting and assurance inspections of nuclear materials are overseen by the EU Commission. The UK has now established its own reporting and inspection regime (including applicable regulations) through the industry regulator (ONR) to comply with International Atomic Energy Agency requirements.

(c) Nuclear fuel ownership

The Euratom Supply Agency (ESA) has the exclusive right to conclude contracts for the supply of nuclear fuel within Euratom member states. While the UK would no longer be bound by the ESA's right to exercise its option over nuclear fuel after it leaves Euratom, that right would still apply to Euratom member states, and a supply to the UK (eg, by France) would constitute an export from the EU, requiring the Commission's authorisation.

The issues set out in this section point to the geographical interdependence of the civil nuclear industry. As the industry transforms from UK designed and built AGRs to a multi-technology fleet of international reactors, the need for international cooperation becomes ever more important.

3.6 The regulated asset base (RAB) model

The government hopes that the RAB model can provide the solution to the thorny problem of new build nuclear funding, as captured in the National Audit Office's somewhat negative analysis of the Hinkley Point C CfD model. The ultimate goal is to bring forward private sector capital (particularly pension and insurance funds) at a lower cost, making the new build project much cheaper than has traditionally been the case.

In its 2019 RAB consultation, the government specifically noted the need to create "a more typical infrastructure investment profile where investor exposure to risks and their returns are bounded". Specifically, the model needed to suit complex development projects with high front-end capital requirements, and very long construction and operation periods (roughly 8–10 and 40–50 years respectively). The RAB model is not widely known, as its use has been limited to monopoly infrastructure assets (power networks, water and gas infrastructure etc). To date, the £4.2 billion Thames Tideway sewer project, which is under construction in London, has been the flagship project for RAB financing.

In its most basic form, a RAB model requires an economic regulator (Regulator) who licenses a developer (Project Co) to operate a regulated project in exchange for a payment from users. The Regulator administers a specific regulatory regime (Economic Regulatory Regime (ERR)), under which costs and risks for the project are apportioned between electricity customers, Project Co and investors. Electricity suppliers are required to raise a levy from their customers (as with existing low-carbon subsidy regimes) which is released in stages by the Regulator to Project Co in accordance with incurred capital expenditure on the project (referred to as Allowed Revenue). Allowed Revenue extends to all approved capital expenditure on the project (including any mandatory costs, such as the funded decommissioning programme), and would be paid over both the construction phase and the operation phase, together with an agreed return on capital (weighted average cost of capital (WACC)). Crucially, the ERR is complemented by an agreed government protection regime against identified "low probability but high impact risk events" (government support package (GSP)).

RAB models differ from the CfD approach used in Hinkley Point C most significantly in relation to the timing of payments to the developer. CfD-supported projects will only receive revenue payments on successful commissioning. This means the up-front development costs (which run into the billions for nuclear projects) and construction costs have to be funded entirely by the developer and its investors. A RAB-funded model is thought to be cheaper because it enables earlier payments to be made to Project Co, generally in line with actual construction of the project. This significantly decreases the cost of capital for the project (because cheaper debt should be available in higher volumes), and the revenue stream also allows the earlier repayment of debt, limiting the impact of compound interest and costs associated with delays to equity returns.

The GSP, in identifying and allocating certain of the key project risks to government (eg, construction cost overrun above a threshold, regulatory and political risk, uninsurable risks and disruption to the debt markets) should also encourage other sources of funding to come forward on a more de-risked (and so, cheaper) basis.

3.7 What next for RAB?

The government's consultation outlined a credible RAB proposal, but it acknowledged that it postponed much of the important detail (particularly around risk apportionment, including construction cost overrun, approvals and payment sequencing) to the detailed design stages, which will entail further consultations. That, together with the brevity of the consultation, created a sense that progress is a little too slow for developers' liking.

It also belies the significant amount of work going on in the background to finance the next round of nuclear projects (the focus here is largely on Sizewell C and, to a lesser extent, Bradwell B). It remains to be seen whether National Grid is being too optimistic in even its scaled-down expectations of the next stage of nuclear deployment. Nonetheless, the government recognises that the key challenges to financing nuclear new build do not just go away with the RAB model – and they acknowledge both the scale of associated capital and the need to find an investable approach to risk-sharing (at an efficient cost), without burdening consumers with risks that should properly sit at development level. That pragmatic approach bodes well for what comes next.

4. Natural gas-fired generation

4.1 Overview

Gas-fired power technology bridges the 'old' and 'new' electricity markets and it will continue to have a crucial role in the energy mix of the future mainstays of global energy. Where it replaces more polluting fuels, it improves air quality and limits emissions of carbon dioxide.[33] As part of the 'dash for gas' in the 1990s, the original role of new build gas plants was to provide baseload power in competition to coal plants, generally through large and more efficient CCGTs. While the archetypal baseload providers at the time were nuclear and coal, gas has now almost entirely displaced coal's market share as it is a significantly cleaner hydrocarbon. This has left coal power plants with the somewhat paradoxical role of flexible market participant, only offering 'peaking' generation when market conditions are favourable (generally when there are high gas prices or high market demand with low renewable availability).

Although the traditional role of gas when built in the 1990s was for baseload output, that role has evolved with the emergence of greater levels of renewable penetration on the system. The 'new' role of natural gas is to provide a flexible, fast response to demand peaks and troughs, filling in the gaps around renewable generation output. This can be delivered by CCGTs operating in frequency response mode or moving from baseload to two-shifting power (ie, coming on twice a

"Gas-fired power technology bridges the 'old' and 'new' electricity markets and it will continue to have a crucial role in the energy mix of the future."

day to meet system demand peaks) or even double two-shifting, but the flexible role is generally more suited to smaller units, referred to as open cycle turbines and peaking plants.

Each mode of gas-fired generation – baseload and flexible – reflects a design-engineered running strategy based upon an assumption of market demand dynamics. To the extent there has been a tipping point, it could be said to be around the advent of the CM. This capacity procurement auction, though technology neutral, was specifically designed to incentivise a new generation of large CCGTs. That has not happened. At about the same time as the CM was introduced, the share of renewable generation on the system started to increase quite significantly.

In a move away from baseload dependency, the market increasingly demands more flexibility and generously rewards units that can provide it. Accordingly, the provision of ancillary services to National Grid (see chapter VIII) is becoming an increasingly valuable revenue stream in its own right, as the wholesale market price stays low and the share of intermittent capacity on the system increases. Natural gas-fired generation has reacted strongly to these market signals.

4.2 Peaking plants

Peaking plants target pockets of high demand, and will operate only for short runs in order to capture temporarily high prices. Typically, this is early in the morning and late in the afternoon (particularly on days with low solar irradiation and low wind) or, more generally, if other large generating units experience unexpected outages and there is a shortfall in supply. As peaking plants are not intended to operate for prolonged periods, it does not make sense to design them to maximise their potential running efficiency (as the higher capital cost would not be compatible with their short run-times). To illustrate this, CCGTs can achieve a thermal efficiency of up to 60% in baseload operation, compared to a single cycle peaking efficiency of around only 40%. Peaking plants are often much smaller in capacity than baseload plant (typically less than 50MW and generally around 20MW) and are generally connected to the distribution network, rather than the transmission network (the networks are described in greater detail in chapter VIII).

4.3 Baseload plants

Baseload plants are typically CCGTs and are designed to operate for long running periods. They have 'combined cycles' in the sense that a steam turbine is added to the gas turbine, so that the energy in the high-temperature exhaust gases from the gas turbine is recaptured by passing the exhaust gas through a heat recovery steam generator (which is essentially a boiler). That generates a number of steam cycles that are passed over high- and low-pressure steam turbine blades, before being condensed and recycled. As mentioned in section 4.1 above, it is possible for CCGTs to operate more flexibly now that market conditions require a different running profile, and turbine manufacturers have been quick to offer a range of flexibility upgrades to allow for faster starts and more flexible ramp ups/downs. However, the consequence of load following and cyclical operation is that, in addition to fuel inefficiencies, the higher number of starts puts more pressure on the turbines and their ancillary equipment. This affects their scheduled maintenance programme and the manufacturer warranties for the turbine (typically both starts and running hours are considered under a CCGT's maintenance agreement). Operators commonly find that cycling or load following in plants that were not designed for that purpose gives rise to a number of issues that have as their cause stresses associated with varying temperatures and pressures, leading to fatigue-related damage (which are not seen to the same extent in baseload operation).

In comparison to small peaking plants, CCGTs are large and generally consist of a number of identical units; for example, three units of a 270MW gas turbine coupled with a secondary 130MW steam turbine. Their size and efficiency mean they also produce far less CO_2, SO_2

and NOx than coal, open-cycle gas turbines and energy from waste (EfW) plants.

In whichever form, gas fired generation is an incredibly important part of the UK energy mix, and the 32GW of installed capacity currently accounts for approximately 40% of electricity generation. Along with interconnectors, demand side response (DSR) and energy storage, gas plants are also a key mitigant to the intermittency of renewable generation.

4.4 The capacity market (CM): a capacity lost?

The CM, as a cornerstone of the EMR initiative, was intended to encourage a new generation of gas-fired power generation. That has not happened for, as it turned out, the increasingly low clearing price of CM contracts proved to be insufficient compensation for falling wholesale power revenue, which made new build gas investment cases very challenging (also not helped, from a capacity perspective, by the ability of interconnectors to participate in the CM). Compounded with the imminent closure of the few remaining coal plants by 2025 and the collapse of two of the three nuclear new build programmes, this has put considerable pressure on the UK's capacity growth and energy security targets.

There are probably two main reasons for the CM not delivering new build gas capacity. The first is supressed market prices and insufficient 'spark spreads' (a measure of gas profitability) to justify the investment case. This has put pressure on plants to compete for ancillary services or in the balancing mechanism (BM), as a way of supplementing their wholesale market income. The second reason is competing government incentives and policies. Almost every other form of power generation was subject to a form of government intervention at or around the same time as the CM was introduced, which has ultimately prejudiced gas' competitiveness. For example, coal was given the option of 'burning out' under a running hours permit before closing, while also benefiting from low coal prices due to increased shale gas production in the US. Nuclear benefited from the strong carbon price top-up to the EU ETS. Renewable generation benefited from a variety of attractive subsidies, including the RO, the FiT and the CfD regime (all of which offer significantly more attractive subsidies than the CM). Ultimately, the combined effect was to push a significant amount of investor interest into renewable generation, rather than gas-fired projects.

4.5 Gas in a renewables world?

As mentioned in section 4.4 above, the CM failed in one of its primary purposes of delivering a new generation of baseload gas-fired power plants. However, the increased share of intermittent renewable generation on the grid has created an opportunity for smaller, flexible peaking plants, which can exploit short-term market price spikes. These spikes in demand are often driven by falling renewable production in cloudy or still conditions.

As the share of intermittent renewable technology grows, so does the need for flexible peaking plants. Peaking plants do not face the same developmental barriers as CCGTs. Large CCGT plants face significant planning costs, mostly driven by the cost of obtaining a development consent order, but are also subject to policy-driven planning costs. These include the requirement to have plans to accommodate carbon capture technology for plants over 300MW. Plants larger than 50MW also have to consider the appropriateness of incorporating CHP technology.

Gas-fired power plants also have to pay a carbon price (to reflect the cost of their associated environmental and emission impacts), which will continue into the future in a post-EU ETS regime. This all points to a somewhat uncertain future for CCGTs but a clear market opportunity for peaking plants. Developers of gas power projects will take great comfort from the endorsement of the role of natural gas in the future energy industry by both the CCC and National Grid –

"Developers of gas power projects will take great comfort from the endorsement of the role of natural gas in the future energy industry by both the CCC and National Grid – although how the very considerable costs of CCUS (including retrofitting to existing generating plant) will fall is still uncertain."

although how the very considerable costs of CCUS (including retrofitting to existing generating plant) will fall is still uncertain.

4.6 Gas: going green?

Aside from peaking plants, there are further interesting opportunities for gas:

(a) Syngas and biogas

Syngas and biogas refer to, respectively, gasification and pyrolysis (for syngas), and anaerobic digestion (for biogas). Syngas is a by-product of gasification or pyrolysis, which is a process where biomass or waste is heated with low oxygen (gasification) or no oxygen (pyrolysis). Biogas is a mixture of carbon dioxide and methane, produced by microorganisms when they digest organic feedstock at low temperatures in anaerobic conditions.

(b) Green hydrogen

Green hydrogen is the production of hydrogen through non carbon-intensive means (electricity produced by renewable technology). Hydrogen could in principle be used as a substitute for natural gas as, when burned, it only produces water vapour. The uncertainty for green hydrogen is the speed and scale at which it can displace natural gas in the UK gas network. This largely depends on the success of pilot projects to both produce hydrogen from sustainable sources (particularly offshore wind farms) and integrate hydrogen into the existing gas network.

The production of syngas and biogas is well advanced technically, but plants are not yet operating at a significant scale. Green hydrogen has far more potential to operate at scale but the associated technology is not as well advanced. The role of CCUS and future applications of hydrogen as an energy carrier are discussed in further detail in chapter VII.

VI. Generation technologies: going from grey to green

1. Overview

The purpose of this chapter is to introduce the two main forms of renewable power generation in the UK: solar and wind. Biomass (the combustion of organic matter as a substitute for conventional fossil fuels) accounts for a significant proportion of electricity generated in the UK (about the same as onshore wind) but, from a technology perspective, many of the principles of coal-fired generation apply. Equally, the policy drivers behind incentivising the conversion of coal plants to biomass have already been discussed in chapter V.

It is also worth saying that categorising biomass as a renewable technology is not without controversy. For example, the European Academies' Science Advisory Council recommend that coal-to-biomass conversions should only be regarded as renewable energy sources in very specific circumstances.[34] In many cases, biomass projects require energy-intensive industrial processes (the harvesting and dehydration of wood in the case of wood pellets, which may involve deforestation where wood pellets are not otherwise made from waste) and incur significant costs and emissions in transporting that fuel to its place of use, often across oceans. Furthermore, the CO_2 previously captured by that organic matter is then released into the atmosphere when combusted, although BECCS attempts to address this, as discussed in chapter VII.

"Solar and wind are the renewable technologies that have seen the greatest level of investment over the past decade, and which hold the greatest promise for a Net Zero-compatible energy mix."

Accordingly, this chapter focuses on solar and wind, which are the renewable technologies that have seen the greatest level of investment over the past decade, and which hold the greatest promise for a Net Zero-compatible energy mix. Some estimates project the need for the UK to source 70–80% of its power from wind and solar power by 2050, a significant extension from the position today.

2. Solar photovoltaic (PV)

2.1 Overview

As mentioned in chapter II, there are two types of solar technology used to generate power: solar photovoltaic (PV) and thermal solar. Solar PV, which is the focus of this chapter, is the generation of power by converting sunlight (solar radiation) into direct current (DC) electricity using semiconductors. When the sun hits the semiconductor within the PV cells, electrons are freed and form an electric current. Solar PV technology is generally employed on a number of panels, either ground- or roof-mounted. In the UK, thermal solar systems are used for direct heating of water or air. Thermal systems can nonetheless be used to generate electricity in more favourable climates by concentrating solar rays in one place so that they are able to heat a fluid to very high temperatures.

2.2 Why solar?

Most available forms of energy ultimately derive from the sun (whether renewable or fossil fuelled). The direct use of solar radiation now tends to be through solar PV which, along with wind, is a fuel-free and increasingly low-cost form of generation. The absence of carbon emissions makes it consistent with the UK's ambition towards carbon neutrality, and the remarkable growth in the UK's investment in solar over the last decade has, in part, allowed the ambitious Net Zero target to be set. For example, the UK's commitment in the first Renewables Energy Directive was for 15% of its total energy requirement to come from renewable sources by 2020 (although the second Renewable Energy Directive has extended the EU's target to 32% by 2030) and under the Climate Change Act (before it was amended) there was a binding commitment to reduce GHGEs by 80% of 1990 levels by 2050. The UK has now become the first major economy to legislate for Net Zero GHGEs by 2050 (this is discussed in greater detail in chapter IV).

Solar can be distributed on a concentrated (solar farms) or distributed (rooftop) basis. It used to be the case that the only real downside to deploying solar was its land-use impact, as solar farms require large surface areas (being around 3.7 acres per MW of installed panels). However, there has been a recognition more recently that solar projects can be effectively paired with agricultural use through principles such as co-cropping, shared grazing and the rotation of land use (which helps to drive lower impact farming methods). From a generation perspective, solar shares the same intermittency challenge as wind, although they have different intermittency profiles depending on whether a minute-by-minute or half-hourly forecast is being used. The extent to which energy storage can address intermittency concerns remains to be seen, but it will play an increasingly important role with recent technological improvements to storage capacity and relaxations to the restrictive storage planning regime.

2.3 Development aspects

Solar is traditionally regarded as having a high capital cost, but low rest-of-life operations and maintenance (O&M) cost. In fact, most solar farms can be operated remotely so it is not even necessary to have a continuous site-based presence to optimise or manage the solar assets. The high capital cost is associated with the cost of components (solar modules, inverters and balance of plant), as otherwise solar farms have short build times and are readily deployable. This means they can be deployed at scale on a relatively non-bespoke basis. However, even this high capital cost has come down rapidly and that reduction has partly justified the government's attitude that solar is a mature technology that can proceed without subsidy support (for new projects). This is discussed further in section

2.6 below. To illustrate the dramatic fall in cost: total solar PV installation cost in the UK decreased in the five years from 2011 to 2016 from circa £2.5 million per MW peak installed to c. £800,000 at the end of 2016 (according to Foresight Group). That has now dropped even further to around £550,000/MW. Of this cost, solar modules accounted for 35–40% of the total installation cost. The factors behind the cost savings are outlined in chapter II and it has been suggested that protectionist import and anti-dumping agendas have provided a constraint to even more significant capital cost reductions.

2.4 Operation aspects

Once constructed, solar farms can generate power for over 30 years, and their low maintenance profile provides an attractive low-risk/high-yield return to investors. As with other generation assets, investors can further optimise the risk profile of their investments by refinancing at any of the key phases of the lifecycle: development, construction and post-commissioning.

2.5 Connection aspects and stranded assets

The connection arrangements form a key part of solar projects. Solar farms are generally connected to the distribution system, meaning they are a category of embedded generation. As such, solar farms require a connection offer from the relevant distribution network operator (DNO) before they become investable. The location of the connection point, the anticipated site load, the extent of connection works (categorised as contestable and non-contestable works) and the integrity of the local grid supply are all fundamental to the nature and cost of the connection offer.

Connection arrangements become particularly important in the context of 'private wire' (also referred to as 'behind the fence') PPAs, as the generator will often be connected directly to the offtaker's property. This will be the case where a solar farm is developed either on the offtaker's property or next to it, so that it can provide a direct source of electricity to that industrial or commercial customer. Where the generator makes use of the offtaker's existing grid connection, the PPA must ensure the generator's connection rights are robust, including that the offtaker is obliged to maintain that connection and comply with the DNO's connection requirements. If this is not thought through carefully, there is a danger that the solar farm could become a 'stranded asset' after the PPA expires or terminates. This means the solar farm will still need the right to connect to the distribution network even without the PPA being in place.

2.6 Solar and subsidy

(a) Subsidy as a stabiliser

Much like onshore wind, the favourable subsidy regime in the last decade has led to an enormous uptake in solar development, and hence an increase in installed solar capacity: from a mere 80MW in 2010 to over 13,300MW by the end of 2019. Of course, improvements in solar technology, particularly in their operating efficiencies in UK temperatures, and the fall in panel costs have also played a significant part in facilitating that expansion. As with other forms of renewable generation, the subsidy available to solar depends both on its installed capacity and the proposed commissioning date. That said, subsidies are now closed to new projects, so they are only relevant in the context of the acquisition and disposal of existing generating sites (where the revenue from the applicable subsidy regime is a fundamental aspect of the overall project value). Some of the observations below on the FiT, RO, CfD and CM schemes were raised initially in chapter IV, but they are discussed here in greater detail specifically in relation to renewable technologies.

(b) Feed-in Tariff (FiT)

The main support mechanism for solar farms is the FiT, which offers

"Once constructed, solar farms can generate power for over 30 years, and their low maintenance profile provides an attractive low-risk/high-yield return to investors."

generators a predictable revenue stream over a 25-year period (in the form of a unit-linked tariff for all electricity generated). This tariff is paid in addition to the wholesale market price and applies to projects of up to 5MW. The early closure of FiTs was forecast in the autumn 2017 budget (when the CfLCL replaced the LCF) and the government subsequently announced (after a quick consultation) the scheme's closure in April 2019. The FiT regime has now been replaced with the SEG, although many commentators are concerned by the lack of revenue certainty offered by the SEG regime.

(c) Renewables Obligation (RO)

The second relevant subsidy arises through the RO on licensed suppliers. The RO gave rise to a tradable market in registered certificates (ROCs) which licensed suppliers can buy from accredited generators (or the secondary market) to satisfy their RO targets. ROCs are awarded to accredited generators (on a banded system dependent on technology) in accordance with the amount of renewable power they generate. If suppliers are unable to provide the necessary number of ROCs, they are required to pay the buy-out price for the shortfall (the 2018–19 RO year had a buy-out price of £47.22/ROC). If suppliers fail to pay the buy-out price by the relevant deadline (31 August) they have defaulted on their RO obligation. While this may arise through cash flow difficulties (the amount due falls at one point in the year, rather than being paid monthly), the more significant cause is suppliers becoming insolvent and exiting the market during the relevant RO year. The relevant shortfall must be made up by the remaining suppliers through a process called mutualisation. The 2018–19 RO year was the second consecutive year that Ofgem triggered mutualisation for the RO (announced in November 2019).

The ROC scheme is now closed to all new generation projects, meaning ROCs are only issued to stations that have existing accreditation. The phase-out of the scheme depended on the technology types. New sub-5MW projects became ineligible for accreditation after April 2017 (the scheme had already become unavailable to solar farms over 5MW from April 2015), although in limited circumstances grace periods applied.

(d) Contracts for Difference (CfD)

The third relevant support mechanism is the CfD regime, which gives CfD holders a guaranteed revenue top-up if the relevant market reference price drops below the applicable CfD strike price (the converse holds for any excess over the strike price). Generators still sell their electricity to the market as usual (generally through a PPA) but the pricing mechanism operates in relation to the difference between the relevant market reference price and the applicable strike price, not the actual price in the PPA. Generators must repay to the CfD contract holder (being the low-carbon contracts company) the difference when the market reference price is higher than the strike price. The purpose of the CfD is therefore to smooth out the generator's revenue, and thus to isolate it from volatile wholesale prices (although this also means there are reduced upside opportunities).

Unlike the FiT and RO, the CfD operates as an auction and so promotes competition between developers to secure a CfD contract at an efficient price. This means that there is a significantly higher risk of obtaining no support under the CfD than the RO (where the eligibility requirements just had to be satisfied). In terms of technologies, offshore wind has been the standout success story for the CfD. Solar, unfortunately, has not had a happy experience. In the first allocation round (AR1), the results of which were announced in February 2015, a total of 27 contracts worth up to £315 million were offered to 2GW of renewable projects. Solar projects only claimed five of these contracts, accounting for 72MW of the 2GW, and only two of the five projects were commissioned as the low strike price did not stack up well against the anticipated installation cost. Onshore wind initially did very well out of AR1 but the position subsequently worsened as both the second (held in 2017) and third auction (in 2019) excluded solar and onshore wind, the government having taken the view that both forms of generation (so-called 'established technologies') were now viable without subsidy support.

(e) Capacity Market (CM)

Unlike the incentive regimes summarised above, the CM is concerned with procuring sufficient firm UK generating capacity to ensure the system is not put under stress in the future (ie, so that in a rolling number of years, there is sufficient supply to meet demand). It is somewhat contentious just how successful the CM has been in delivering this purpose. Projects cannot receive subsidies through more than one regime, so RO, FiT and CfD participants cannot also participate in the CM (to prevent double recovery and unfairly loading consumer bills). There has been a long-running question over the appropriateness of non-subsidised renewable generation participating in the CM. The debate has centred on how to answer the problem of intermittency (which is the opposite of the CM's drive for firm capacity). This means deciding an appropriate handicap for non-dispatchable technology (referred to as de-rating).

In mid-2019, the government confirmed that the replacement T-3 auction in early 2020 (for delivery year 2022/23) would, for the first time, allow certain non-subsidised renewable technologies to participate. Participation was to be on the basis of an "equivalent firm

"Although not strictly speaking a subsidy or public support mechanism, the approach to allocating transmission network operating and system balancing costs has led to a number of significant benefits for generators who are connected to the distribution network."

capacity de-rating methodology", to reflect renewables' intermittent nature as against 'firm' generation. The purpose of de-rating is to get a figure that is equivalent to firm generation – that is, can be compared with other participating technologies. In addressing this question of intermittency, the government believed that allowing the participation of (appropriately de-rated) renewable technology does not increase the security of supply risk, but simply alters where and how its contribution to security of supply is accounted for, while upholding the technology-neutral principle of the CM.

The issue will be, of course, whether the de-rating handicap on top of already record-low clearing prices will be sufficiently attractive for renewables to counterbalance both the CM's participation obligations and the penalty risk of failing to deliver during a system stress event. 547MW of merchant renewable projects (11 onshore wind and one solar project) prequalified for the 2020 T-3 auction, which was typically competitive with 61GW prequalified capacity competing against a procurement target of only 44GW. To give an indication of the effect of de-rating, that 547MW of prequalified renewable capacity was de-rated to a mere 42.5MW of new build capacity. It was a similar story for the 2020 T-4 auction where 704MW of onshore wind and solar prequalified capacity was de-rated to only 50MW. The low de-rating capacity for renewable technologies highlights the fact that CM revenue will not come anywhere close to replacing the lost FiT and RO subsidies.

(f) Embedded benefits

Although not strictly speaking a subsidy or public support mechanism, the approach to allocating transmission network operating and system balancing costs has led to a number of significant benefits for generators who are connected to the distribution network (referred to as 'embedded generators' and therefore 'embedded benefits'). With increasing levels of renewables power being developed, the proportion of embedded generation is increasing. Embedded benefits are currently subject to a comprehensive price review by Ofgem under the Target Charging Review, the expectation being that they will be significantly reduced, and in some cases (particularly the allocation of balancing services use of system (BSUoS) charges), made a cost rather than a benefit. The main categories of embedded benefits for distribution-connected (or embedded) generators have included:

- **Triad benefits or transmission network use of system charges (TNUoS):** These charges are the avoided costs of not using the transmission system during the so-called triad periods. Triad refers to the three half-hour settlement periods between November and February with the highest system demand, and is used in the determination of TNUoS charges.
- **Balancing services use of system (BSUoS) charges:** BSUoS is a charge that National Grid ESO (as the system operator) levies on BM participants for the costs of operating the BM and procuring other ancillary services. If embedded generators do not participate in the BM, they do not pay BSUoS charges.
- **Avoided transmission losses:** Depending on the location of the embedded generation (which as a general presumption, is much closer to the point of consumption than traditional transmission-connected plants), projects could avoid the potentially very costly energy losses associated with transporting electricity from the place of generation to the place of consumption.

2.7 Solar without subsidy

The UK has already seen subsidy-free solar farms. The first to operate without subsidy support was Clayhill solar farm, commissioned in September 2017. That project was able to exploit the falling cost of solar panels and achieve operating efficiencies through co-locating with battery storage, thus avoiding the majority of the grid connection cost. It therefore became something of a trophy case in response to widespread criticism at the time about the timing and speed of the FiT and ROC closures. Looking ahead to a subsidy-free world, the continued growth of the solar market will depend on the following factors:

(a) Revenue optimisation

As public subsidies are phased out, the energy price in the PPA becomes far more important to the overall project revenue. As such, corporate PPAs and 'within the fence' or 'direct wire' PPAs are likely to continue to be popular. Direct wire PPAs, in particular, often allow a price to be secured which is actually above the wholesale market price, but is still less for the offtaker than taking power from the grid. This is because directly supplied electricity does not also include the grid charges and non-energy costs that an offtaker would otherwise pay to a licensed supplier (which make up a considerable part of the energy bill). In contrast, a limited offtake market has seen the price of corporate PPAs fall below the market price, but they remain attractive to generators because of the long-term price certainty they provide.

(b) Lower finance costs

Successful non-subsidised projects will have slim margins so it is important to have competitive financing costs (referred to as the cost of capital). This can be optimised according to both the nature of the project development stage and its attendant risk profile, and may take the form of corporate loans, third-party debt, equity injections or local funding campaigns (in each case exploiting the reliable yield of solar farms to decrease the loan risk profile).

(c) Reducing component, installation and operating costs

This will be achieved in a number of ways, including through:

- continued research and development in solar cell technology;
- competition in the supply chain; achieving lower rents in the property lease;
- finding economies of scale in portfolio development;
- standardising installation costs; and
- driving lower asset management and maintenance costs (perhaps through efficiencies in aggregating portfolios of sites).

The factors outlined in this section have all contributed to the government's decision to remove ROCs, FiTs and CfD support from solar development. Irrespective of developers' preferences, projects have now been forced to accept subsidy-free solar as the new norm. Optimising revenues in this new world is fundamental and will continue to incentivise inventiveness, as already being seen in the co-location of solar with on-site battery storage capacity and the emergence of hybrid generation projects.

3. Wind power

3.1 Overview

As with solar generation, wind power is a fuel-free and increasingly low-cost form of high-volume electricity generation. Unlike with solar generation, the UK has amongst the best wind resources in the world, and so has been able to invest heavily in this sector over the last decade (particularly in offshore wind). Originally perceived as being expensive to develop, at least for offshore wind which faced a number of engineering challenges, there are now almost no significant downsides to wind-powered generation. Wind, much like solar, does not have the legacy waste issues associated with nuclear, nor the enduring environmental and GHGE issues of coal- and gas-fired generation. Public opposition to inflated energy bills is now largely in check, as new subsidy support is conditional on a significant reduction in legacy costs under the government's new control for low-carbon levies.

As mentioned in section 2.6 above, for solar, it is now effectively government policy that onshore wind can proceed without policy support, and that offshore wind should operate at very modest levels of support. The latter is reflected in projects being prepared to accept CfD contracts at prices materially below wholesale market prices.

"Unlike with solar generation, the UK has amongst the best wind resources in the world, and so has been able to invest heavily in this sector over the last decade (particularly in offshore wind). Originally perceived as being expensive to develop, at least for offshore wind which faced a number of engineering challenges, there are now almost no significant downsides to wind-powered generation."

Photo 4. Teesside Offshore Wind Farm

Source: © Brian Matthews, published with permission

Unsurprisingly then, wind is playing an increasingly important role in the global energy mix. Also, the UK is leading the way in offshore wind development.

3.2 Wind in the UK

UK wind generation hit a record high of over 16GW one stormy weekend in December 2019, which at the time accounted for well over 40% of UK electricity supply (it accounts for around 17% of the UK generation mix normally). Wind output exceeded coal output for the first time in 2016 and the UK now has a total installed capacity of over 23GW. Incredibly, the UK has more installed offshore wind capacity than any other country.

Of that total wind capacity, there are far more onshore wind projects by number but, due to planning restrictions, they have smaller turbine capacities. Also, since the removal of RO support for onshore turbines in 2016 and the effective moratorium on the granting of planning consents in the UK, the number of planning applications for onshore wind projects has dropped massively. Onshore projects still account for around 14GW of installed capacity – broadly equivalent to 10 nuclear plants or seven large coal stations.

Offshore wind accounts for fewer projects but higher turbine capacities, with load factors approximately 30% higher than onshore wind turbines. There is around 9GW of installed capacity of offshore projects and, according to the Crown Estate, a development pipeline of around 24GW. As with other forms of renewable generation, offshore wind has seen significant growth over the last decade – moving from around 0.8% of the UK generation mix in 2010 to 10% by 2020. The government launched its Offshore Wind Sector Deal in March 2019, under which it announced an ambition to generate a third of its electricity from offshore wind by 2030, targeting 30GW of capacity. Even this lofty ambition now looks modest in light of Boris Johnson's December 2019 general election pledge to increase the level of offshore capacity to 40GW by 2030.

3.3 Cost of wind

(a) Onshore vs offshore

With the exception of the 15 onshore wind projects that were awarded Round 1 CfD contracts (which together only accounted for 750MW of capacity), the main support mechanism for onshore wind is the RO. The RO underpins around a quarter of current UK generating capacity, being approximately 30GW. Onshore wind is by far the largest benefactor of this support, accounting for 12.5GW of capacity. Unfortunately, the RO regime for new onshore wind closed in April 2016 and onshore wind has also been excluded from both the second and third rounds of the CfD auction. As mentioned in section 2.6(e) above, like solar, onshore wind has until very recently not been able to participate in the CM. This means new onshore wind projects (prior to the 2020 T-3 CM auction) have not qualified for policy support, which has been a major issue in the industry as onshore developers have been left in limbo while they see the offshore market take off.

Like solar, the reason behind the withdrawal of policy support is that onshore wind has the lowest LCOE of any UK generating technology, if carbon price support is applied to conventional thermal projects. This lower cost is explained by many of the same factors outlined above in the solar section. Nonetheless, there are diminishing marginal returns to be delivered from wind generation; the trend towards ever reducing technology costs has started to plateau, and even reverse for some components and projects, partly due to manufacturing and shipping costs arising through environmental levies (eg, sulphur taxation). Continued cost reductions are thus dependent on being able to use a smaller number of larger turbines to deliver the same project nameplate capacity, but this is not particularly encouraged by the current planning regime.

A particularly important cost efficiency for offshore projects is the emergence of more sophisticated preventative maintenance regimes.

This includes the use of predictive fault analysis and remote monitoring to minimise costly human intervention if things go wrong. Offshore wind has also been able to capture significant cost savings through the deployment of larger and more efficient turbines (unconstrained by the onshore planning regime). Considering the largest onshore wind turbines are no more than 3.5MW (although 5MW turbines are in the pipeline), this difference is very marked: Orsted's new Hornsea 1 wind farm (120 kilometres off the Yorkshire coast) is using 7 MW turbines, each a towering 190 metres high.

But even the 7MW turbines now look modest in comparison to plans announced in late 2019 for the Dogger Bank Wind Farms (a 50:50 joint venture between Equinor and SSE Renewables). The Dogger Bank Wind Farms comprise three 1.2GW projects that were all successful in the 2019 third round CfD (AR3). When built, they will become the world's largest offshore wind farm (first generation is anticipated in 2023) and will feature GE Renewable Energy's new Haliade-X turbines. These are the industry's first 12MW offshore turbines, making them the most powerful wind turbines in the world (with a quite remarkable leading capacity factor of 63%). They are monumental structures: each one is 260 metres high: 80% as high as the Eiffel Tower.[35]

Figure 16: Scale of the Haliade-X

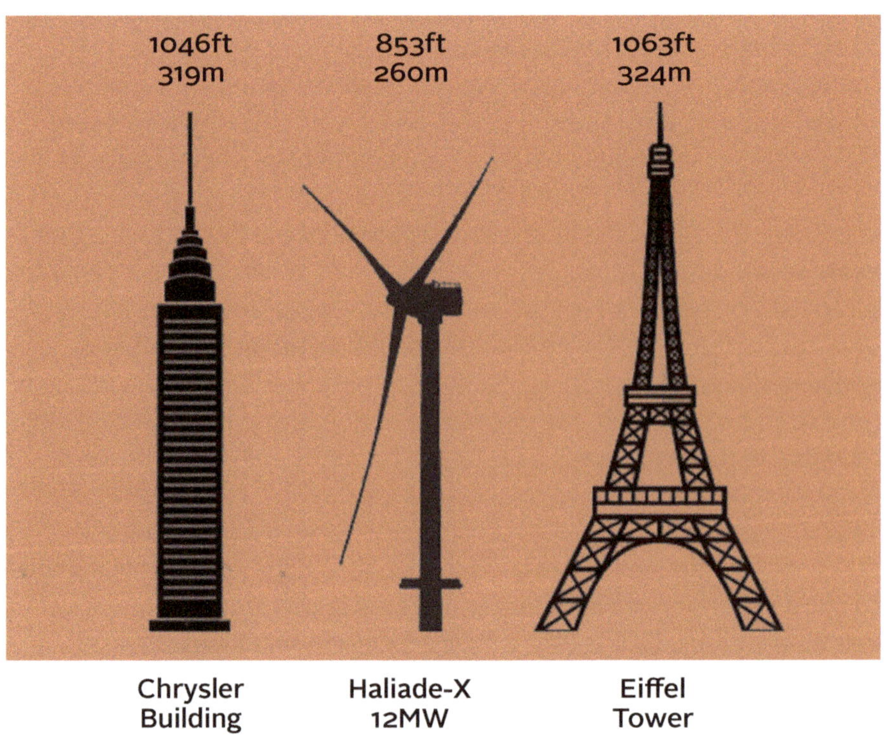

(b) Offshore and the Contracts for Difference (CfD)
Unlike onshore wind, offshore wind can still compete for support under the CfD, as it is regarded as a 'less established' technology. There is a slight exception to this onshore/offshore dichotomy: in the recent AR3, 'remote island wind' was allowed to participate, albeit at a much higher administrative strike price than offshore wind, which reflects the perceived lack of competiveness for that technology.

AR3 produced the lowest CfD prices to date and was particularly contentious because of its exclusion of 'established' in favour of 'less established' technologies (which ruled out mainland onshore wind and solar). Administrative strike prices before the auction provided a cap to control outturn cost, in this case (for offshore wind) at £56/MWh for 2023–24 projects and £53/MWh for projects delivered in 2024–25. By comparison, the AR2 (2017) Hornsea 2 and Moray Offshore projects were awarded £57.50/MWh strike prices (for 2022–23 delivery) and the Triton Knoll project was awarded a £74.75 contract (for 2021–22 delivery). Round 1 saw two offshore projects average £117/MWh clearing prices.

As it turned out, savings against the administrative prices were significant for AR3: offshore wind cleared at £39.65/MWh for 2023–24 projects, a massive 29% saving over the admin price, and at £41.6/MWh for 2024–25 projects, a similar 21% saving over the admin price (in both cases in 2012 prices). In total, 5.77GW of capacity was awarded to 12 projects (two advanced conversion technologies, four remote island wind and six offshore wind projects). Remote island wind won contracts for the first time in a CfD auction (obtaining 257MW of capacity), and outturn was comfortably within the applicable 6GW auction capacity cap (the first time a capacity cap has been used). Offshore wind took 95% of awarded capacity, with island wind taking the majority of the remaining 5%.

3.4 Investing in wind power
The wind sector is now mature from an investment perspective. Its growth has been facilitated by its relative attractiveness to pension and infrastructure funds, who weigh the long-term finance commitment against the low and stable returns such projects offer. In this respect, express government policy support is fundamental to maintaining investment viability for such long-term projects – particularly as offshore CfD strike prices move closer to, and even under, projected wholesale market prices. Aside from the regulatory and policy commitment they reflect, government contracts provide important revenue stability over the tenor of a CfD contract. It is this revenue stabilisation that is particularly important to investors, as it de-risks offshore investment from volatile short-term and hard-to-forecast long-term market prices (particularly in the context of price

cannibalisation concerns, discussed further below). The net effect of de-risking the revenue aspects of a project is a lower cost of capital. As with solar, the cost of capital is a very significant part of the overall cost of a wind project.

There is now a considerable opportunity to invest in wind projects, as the scale of the low-carbon capacity challenge has been realised. As outlined in chapter IV, National Grid's 2019 Future Energy Scenarios forecast that to deliver Net Zero, total installed generation capacity in the UK would have to more than double from 106GW to 263GW by 2050. This massive increase in capacity assumes a six-fold increase in offshore wind generation (from 2018 levels). This is remarkable considering there is only around 53GW of low-carbon capacity installed today (which includes nuclear). Bridging that gap is quite an investment challenge, as 263GW is over six times the capacity already delivered under the combined low-carbon support regimes (ie, the RO, FiT and CfD). On top of that, the existing 53GW of low-carbon capacity will have exceeded its economic life by 2050 and so will also require replacing or repowering (for which there is no existing favourable policy or planning regime).

In short, a generating unit in 2050 will not have existed in 2020, and will be part of a fleet that is vastly bigger than the generating fleet of 2020. National Grid anticipates that wind will be the largest contributor to installed electricity generation capacity in 2050, with natural gas CCUS and solar some way behind. The existing CfD and planning regime will require significant expansion if this is to prove a realistic expectation. In September 2019 the Crown Estate announced the opening of Offshore Wind Leasing Round 4, which created the opportunity for at least 7GW of new seabed rights for offshore wind development around England and Wales. It is unlikely, though, that 7GW of seabed rights for projects likely to commission in the late 2020s will be enough, in light of these ambitious targets. Equally, even assuming the CfD continues to offer sufficient incentive for offshore development, there is no investment-attractive policy support for new onshore wind. The same holds true for existing onshore projects when their subsidy support schemes expire.

There is a second investment concern for wind projects. The increasing proportion of non-dispatchable renewable generation on the system gives rise to an effect known as 'price cannibalisation', which over the long term has an erosive effect on wholesale market prices. Price cannibalisation occurs when 'must dispatch' technology (mainly wind and solar, as these are fuel-free technologies with no marginal cost of dispatch) creates an over-supply on the system during very windy or sunny conditions, and this oversupply pushes down wholesale market power prices. That depressive effect is

"There is a second investment concern for wind projects. The increasing proportion of non-dispatchable renewable generation on the system gives rise to an effect known as 'price cannibalisation', which over the long term has an erosive effect on wholesale market prices."

magnified by the greater proportion of renewable capacity on the system relative to other technologies. This was demonstrated reasonably publicly in May 2019, when UK power prices turned negative for nine consecutive hours due to a combination of shortfall in demand (2GW below forecasts) and high levels of wind generation (which provided almost 40% of demand). During this period, wholesale power prices fell to -£71.26/MWh, requiring National Grid ESO to pay over £6.6 million in balancing costs (compared to just £300,000 the day before), demonstrating in one 24-hour period the volatility introduced by high capacity intermittent generation. The same thing happened during a stormy weekend in December 2019 when wind output exceeded 16GW (comfortably over 40% of supply), although this also led, for the first time in the UK, to negative day ahead prices.

The investment challenge for wind is, therefore, whether the triumvirate of, first, decreasing technology costs; second, improved operating efficiencies; and third, potential synergies of co-located energy storage, can outweigh the two challenges of wholesale market price cannibalisation and finance providers' conservative attitude to short-term market price volatility. The latter consideration requires an institutional mind shift: investors traditionally look at long-term revenue stability to underwrite the business case for a project. Increasingly, renewable projects will make their revenue in the short-term balancing and spot markets, meaning that, like solar, wind may have to survive on a merchant basis in a post-subsidy world. Long-term corporate PPAs will remain attractive, but this is still a small market with poor liquidity in the offtaker pool, not helped by the challenge of offering an appropriate credit rating to underwrite the revenue stream for the project. Accepting this lack of revenue certainty is fundamental to the continued growth of the wind sector. It is hard to see that the cost of capital will continue to fall if that challenge is not properly addressed.

3.5 Wind: finance aspects

It is far from breaking news that onshore wind projects have some significant issues to overcome before the capacity gap summarised above can be closed. The loss of subsidy revenue is a concern, but as mentioned already, it is more likely to be the lack of revenue stability that will affect the bankability of grid-scale onshore wind. Even if long-term wholesale power prices offer investable returns, banks and infrastructure investors still require protection around short-term volatility. There has been some interesting commentary about the traditional debt-finance model not sitting well with the policy support-free onshore projects. This is primarily because three- or six-monthly amortising loan repayments (capital and interest) are normally paid in accordance with a pre-agreed repayment schedule, irrespective of short-term project cashflow challenges arising from a dip in power prices. This means projects without CfD support will have very little tolerance to debt repayment defaults, and the associated collateral related steps that could initiate for the debt lender. Relatedly, thin or negative margins around volatile market revenue could impact the debt service cover ratio, as (when the power price dips) there would be insufficient revenue over the debt service requirement.

Such issues do not exist to the same extent with ROC-accredited or CfD projects, as they have a long-term guaranteed and stable revenue source on top of wholesale market prices (or in support of a strike price). The concern is that debt providers will either lend less or at a higher cost, in response to these challenges.

In light of the issues noted above, there have been several proposals to modify the CfD (as the most acceptable existing support mechanism) to reincorporate a wider range of technologies and to unblock the pipeline of projects that are currently looking somewhat despondently at their business cases. One suggestion has been to adjust the strike price to a CfD floor. The purpose of the floor is to create the revenue certainty required by investors and to thereby lower the cost of capital for the wind development pipeline. The floor guarantees the onshore wind project is not exposed to market prices below a certain level (ie, it gives investors protection to volatility), but the consumer is not excessively prejudiced by a pass-through of costs as the level of support is more modest than with a strike price. Similarly, there have been proposals to allow the CfD counterparty to repay any 'subfloor top up' before it can enjoy any subsequent upside over the floor when prices recover.

Outside the CfD, challenges around setting a satisfactory de-rating factor and the difficulties in applying the existing penalty regime to intermittent or non-dispatchable technology have made it difficult for renewables to participate in the CM. In 2019 the government confirmed that the replacement T-3 auction in early 2020 (for delivery year 2022/23) will allow certain renewable technologies to participate, and this is discussed further in section 2.6(e) of this chapter.

VII. Net Zero and future technologies

1. Overview

Chapters V and VI offered an overview of the gradual transition from a conventional energy system (dominated by coal and gas) to a low-carbon one (dominated by solar, wind and firm low-carbon power). It is commonly accepted that the choice is not a binary one. For example, as mentioned in chapter VI, wind generation recently reached a record-breaking 16GW, well in excess of 40% of supply at the time, which led to the longest period of negative pricing in the BM and, for the first time in the UK, negative day-ahead prices. These records rightly initiated a flurry of excited commentary on the sector news sites, particularly from people who were essentially being paid to charge their cars and do their laundry overnight. And yet, only three days later, those few coal stations that are still open were generating at a level well above both solar and wind combined. It is a topsy turvy industry.

With that in mind, the fundamental challenge of delivering Net Zero is in quickly finding ways to decarbonise electricity and to electrify more of our energy consumption. This will allow the UK to meet a growing global energy demand in a way that is compatible with the Paris Agreement, as set out in chapters II and IV. Some of the technologies that will facilitate this outcome were discussed briefly in chapter IV. This chapter sets out in more detail a perspective on the respective contributions to be offered by energy storage, floating wind, hydrogen, carbon capture technology (including 'negative emissions') and advanced (or 'small') nuclear.

2. Energy storage

2.1 Overview

The requirement for energy storage capacity is central to any future projection of a Net Zero-compatible energy mix. In National Grid's Future Energy Scenarios 2019 (FES 2019), it forecast a need for a significant increase in electricity storage capacity to support the intermittent output from renewables and a move away from conventional baseload technology. That transition is already well under way – in the year leading up to FES 2019, 50 storage projects were commissioned in the UK, providing around 500MW of capacity. Most of these were short-duration lithium-ion batteries (often housed in shipping container-like structures), but they also included new storage technologies, including a liquid air facility.

2.2 Opportunities: co-location and revenue stacking

The two key, non-technical, opportunities for energy storage are the ability to successfully co-locate with generating technologies ('co-location') and the ability to source multiple income streams in a post-subsidy world ('revenue stacking'). Co-location allows the smoothing of a project's generation profile, potentially allowing it to optimise its offtake arrangements and/or access other markets (eg, a battery paired with solar could access frequency response and reserve markets, whereas solar on its own probably could not). There is a noticeable trend towards a presumption of co-location for future onshore projects for this reason. Most co-located projects are battery storage with solar or wind, but battery has also been successfully co-located with gas, hydro and tidal projects. There are a lot of natural synergies for co-location beyond simply smoothing the generation profile, including making use of an existing grid connection point.

A bottleneck in a long pipeline of storage projects was created by the need to stack multiple revenue streams to make a project commercially viable. There are a range of options open to developers but they do not typically offer the revenue certainty required by debt funders. Example revenue sources include price arbitrage in the wholesale or balancing markets, and offering ancillary services (particularly frequency response services). These types of services, and their importance to National Grid, are discussed in greater detail in chapter VIII.

It is also important to be aware that the emergence of residential storage technologies allows domestic customers to pair a 'behind the meter' battery with rooftop solar PV, to reduce domestic network-

Photo 5. 49MW grid-scale battery, at the West Burton B site

Source: © Brian Matthews, published with permission

supplied consumption and to provide services to the grid. This is because installing a domestic battery (to store surplus power from the solar panels in sunny conditions) reduces the customer's exposure to more expensive electricity tariffs (which carry non-power-related costs), and also allows the customer to optimise price movements by importing grid-supplied power when prices are low, or exporting when prices are high. There are also exciting opportunities emerging around using block trading and consolidating a network of batteries to create virtual power stations and energy markets.

A brief overview of existing and developing energy storage technologies is provided in the next section.

2.3 Battery storage – lithium ion and electric vehicles (EVs)

Many of the commercial opportunities for grid-scale battery storage are set out in chapter VIII. Battery technology consists of electrochemical cells that convert stored chemical energy into electrical energy. Each battery cell has a positive terminal (cathode) and a negative terminal (anode), and electrolytes allow ions to move between the terminals, enabling a current to flow out of the battery.

The leading battery storage technology is lithium ion (although there are many others, including redox flow). The purpose of grid-scale batteries is to provide fast reserve and frequency response services, as batteries can generally respond within seconds of a system call. Most such batteries have capacities of up to 49MW but some larger projects are now coming forward.

Lithium ion is also the prevailing technology for EVs. As mentioned in chapter IV, the growth of EVs is crucial to the decarbonisation of the transport sector, but the charging behaviour of these EVs also presents an opportunity to help balance system demand and provides access to a new category of distributed energy storage. National Grid (in FES 2019) anticipates that 35 million EVs could be on the road in 2050, so the charging dynamics of this very high number of batteries will provide useful system flexibility (through 'smart charging', which is choosing when and where to charge). It will also facilitate the integration of a higher level of renewable generation onto the system, as output can be stored on a distributed basis during periods of high output. National Grid anticipates that the smart charging of vehicles could enable the storage of approximately 20% of the UK's solar generation. Continued advances in technology and materials have significantly increased the density, reliability and output of modern battery systems. Economies of scale and competition in the supply chain have dramatically reduced their cost.[36]

2.4 Pumped storage

The most prevalent form of energy storage globally is pumped hydroelectric, which provides utility-scale storage using simple gravity-based technology. Pumped hydroelectric facilities store energy in the form of water in an upper geological reservoir. During periods of high electricity demand, power can be generated by allowing the stored water in the upper reservoir to cascade to a lower reservoir. As the water falls it drives turbines in the same manner as conventional hydropower stations. When demand is low and the cost of electricity falls, the water is pumped back up to the upper reservoir using the cheaper electricity. The commercial principle is therefore simple: gravity is used to time arbitrage the delivery of power, electricity can be generated when prices are high, but when prices are low electricity can be consumed to pump the water to the upper reservoir, ready for the next period of high prices or demand. The difference between the two, very approximately, determines the profitability of the plant.

From a grid management perspective, pumped hydroelectric provides a very valuable mechanism to balance demand ('load') on the system, as unlike many forms of fuel-fired power stations, electricity can be produced almost immediately by releasing the water from the upper reservoir. Hydroelectric facilities tend to be very capital intensive in the build phase, and obviously rely on an appropriate geological site (in the UK this limits them to a handful of locations in Wales and Scotland).

The principles behind pumped storage can apply to other storage mediums and facilities, for example liquid air or compressed air can be stored in pressurised containers or in salt caverns. In the case of liquid air storage, air is cooled so that it liquefies and can then be stored in pressurised vessels. Compressed air can be stored under pressure (generally in underground salt caverns) and, when power is required, the compressed air can be heated so that it expands and drives a turbine next to the wellhead on the surface.

2.5 Thermal storage

Most of the references in this report to solar concern photovoltaic solar (PV), but thermal solar plants are an effective means of capturing thermal energy from the sun which can then be stored until required (in contrast, PV uses the sun's energy to generate electricity in PV panels). The excess solar energy produced during peak sunlight hours can be stored in thermal storage facilities alongside the solar panels, including in the form of molten salt. The stored thermal energy in the molten salt can be extracted when needed, for example, in the evening or at night to help generate steam, which drives a turbine to produce electricity.

Although liquid air storage is described under pumped storage above, essentially the same principles apply for liquid storage in reverse to

"The most prevalent form of energy storage globally is pumped hydroelectric, which provides utility-scale storage using simple gravity-based technology."

the storage of thermal energy (the substance is cooled and when power is required, brought back to a gaseous state, driving a turbine to produce electricity).

2.6 Hydrogen storage

The possibility of using hydrogen as an inter-seasonal storage carrier is described in section 4 below.

3. Floating wind power

3.1 Overview

As part of the Net Zero ambition, the UK anticipates offshore wind playing a leading role in delivering the considerable additional capacity of renewable energy required, alongside other renewable and firm capacity technologies. The opportunities for higher concentrations of conventional offshore wind become limited by sea depths of greater than 50 metres. This means the North Sea, the US's West Coast and Japan, all of which have deep offshore waters and high wind capacity, are looking very closely at floating wind. A recent report by RenewableUK and Scottish Renewables suggested that floating wind could be cost-competitive with other technologies by 2030 (based on realistic levels of investment) and that the UK floating offshore wind sector can deliver around £34 billion in economic benefits by 2050, with the export market alone being worth at least £230 million a year by 2031.[37]

3.2 Early stage technology

This is a pivotal moment for the floating offshore wind sector. Although floating structures are still in the early development phase, two UK projects have demonstrated the considerable promise of the sector. The first is EDF Renewables' Blyth offshore demonstrator wind farm (6 kilometres off the coast of Blyth in Northumberland), which commissioned in 2017. The Blyth project contains five 8.3MW turbines and is the first offshore wind farm to deploy 'float and submerge' technology. The project's purpose is to demonstrate the cheaper construction and installation costs associated with towing gravity-based foundations to the project site, where they can subsequently be submerged to the seabed (in place of traditional piled foundations). The other advantage of gravity base over piled foundations is that they can be deployed close to shore without installation noise issues.

The second project is a 'true' floating one and has already proved stable enough to withstand strong offshore winds and storms. It has also demonstrated higher than average capacity factors for offshore wind. That is Equinor's Hywind project, 25 kilometres off the coast of Aberdeen in sea depths of up to 130 metres. Hywind consists of five 6MW turbines (a 30MW project), and is installed on a spar buoy foundation (which are steel cylinders filled with a ballast). Although a floating structure, the foundation extends approximately 80 metres below the surface and is attached to the seabed by a three-point mooring. These are big pieces of kit: the overall structure is 255 metres (from spar-base to maximum blade tip height). Impressively for the UK offshore sector, Hywind has become the world's first commercial floating wind project.

More recently, EDP Renewable's WindFloat Atlantic wind farm has also started supplying the Portuguese grid with power. That project, which commissioned in early January 2020, comprises three separate platforms of 8.4MW turbines, making them the world's largest turbines installed on a floating platform.

3.3 Crown Estate and floating projects

The Crown Estate launched the UK's first major offshore wind leasing round in a decade in late 2019 (Round 4). This opened up the opportunity for at least 7GW of new seabed rights for offshore wind development in the waters around England and Wales. Importantly, Round 4 identified the need to facilitate and unlock opportunities for innovation, including floating wind. The Crown Estate drew particular attention to the need to incentivise pre-commercial testing and the successful demonstration of floating offshore wind farms.

The Crown Estate also run an Offshore Wind Test and Demonstration programme. Under that project, the Crown Estate allows certain seabed access rights for the testing and demonstration of emerging offshore wind technologies, including floating wind. This is limited to projects of up to 100MW capacity and only applies to technologies that have not previously been deployed commercially.

3.4 Floating wind as a sector opportunity

The technically exploitable potential of floating wind power in Europe is hard to forecast accurately. The European Wind Energy Association (EWEA) forecast that by 2050, offshore wind capacity in Europe could reach 460GW. This can only be achieved by accessing deep water sites (those greater than 50 metres), which requires the deployment of floating technology.[38] The potential of the sector is considerable though – the EWEA also believes that energy produced from turbines in deep North Sea waters could meet the EU's total electricity consumption four times over. The RenewableUK report referred to above takes a somewhat more practical approach, but still believes that the UK has the potential to install 75GW of offshore wind capacity (including floating wind) by 2050, up from 8.5GW now. As outlined in chapter IV, the UK has an ambition of multiplying its existing capacity of low-carbon generation by at least a factor of four by 2050 and,

"Conventional offshore projects are only feasible at depths of up to 50–60 metres. By several estimates, this means 80% of Europe's offshore wind resources are inaccessible for conventional bottom-fixed turbines."

under the 2019 Offshore Wind Sector Deal, procuring 30GW of offshore wind capacity by 2030. This target did not last long, having been rapidly upgraded during the 2019 General Election campaign to a revised ambition of 40GW by 2030.

3.5 Floating wind benefits

There are a number of benefits in promoting floating technology to support the continued growth of the offshore wind market:

- **Sector growth:** Conventional offshore projects are only feasible at depths of up to 50–60 metres. By several estimates, this means 80% of Europe's offshore wind resources are inaccessible for conventional bottom-fixed turbines. Floating structures therefore give turbines the ability to generate power a long way offshore.
- **Operating efficiencies:** Deep-water environments allow better asset optimisation and optimal turbine spacing, due to stronger and more consistent winds. Small increases in speed result in large increases in energy production, for example, a turbine in a 15 mph wind can generate double the energy of one in a 12 mph wind.[39] This gives the opportunity for increased yield and capacity factors at a competitive LCOE.
- **Ease of installation:** Floating structures avoid the need to cast

solid foundations or use the kind of specialist construction vessels required for fixed offshore wind turbines. They are therefore less intrusive to the seabed and, in principle, they are also less exposed to volatility in the steel market. They have the additional advantage of being constructed on shore and towed to their installation site.

- **Visual impact:** Floating structures can be located between 15–22 kilometres from the coast, thereby minimising their visual and maritime impact.

3.6 Key issues with floating projects

The technical, commercial and legal risks associated with offshore wind development generally are now well understood. The following issues are particularly important for floating projects:

- **Technical specification:** During installation, there are additional technical challenges associated with mounting the steel structures (which can be 200 metres long) to their anchors and (extremely heavy) chains.
- **Minimising movement:** Turbine efficiency is reduced if wave action allows floating turbines to move too much. This negates some of the benefits of wind being more stable over open sea.
- **Demonstration technology:** Floating wind is still largely in demonstration stage (albeit with a positive early track record). There are therefore the usual risks associated with first-of-a-kind technology. To a very large extent, this is mitigated by the deep offshore oil and gas and wind experience over the past few decades. In fact, the UK is uniquely placed to benefit from its long track record in the North Sea oil and gas industry.
- **Maintenance costs:** Offshore O&M costs are already greater than for onshore projects, and there is the potential for them to be even higher for floating turbines that are further out to sea, with greater wave heights making access challenging. However, it may be that some floating projects can be towed to shore for major maintenance (eg, nacelle or blade repair or replacement). As with offshore wind more generally, preventative maintenance and remote monitoring are key.
- **Environmental and shipping:** The large blade sweep creates a potential hazard for birds, meaning floating farms cannot be placed in areas where there are large bird migrations. The same point applies to shipping lanes, given the sector's dependency on far offshore locations.
- **Decommissioning strategy:** Early trials, for example, by Equinor and Principle Power, indicate that floating farms should be easier than bottom-mounted turbines to decommission. This is because they can be unhitched from their moorings and towed onshore for controlled dismantling.

3.7 What next for floating wind?

Momentum is growing rapidly in this embryonic sector and it has quickly gathered support across developers, trade associations and research institutions. For example, in late 2019 the University of Strathclyde published a report which made five recommendations to support the market's growth.[40] Foremost amongst these was the plea for government to introduce a new long-term subsidy regime for floating wind projects (and where possible, to preserve access to EU demonstration funds). From an investor's perspective, this would offer a guaranteed level of subsidy over a long period, which would go some way to mitigating some of the risks of this being (relatively) new technology. The report, like many in the industry, recommends the introduction of a new 'innovation-oriented' CfD pot for pre-commercial technologies, which would entail minimal disturbance to the existing support arrangements.

As more of the traditional offshore developers look to floating technology, this sector should present reason for considerable optimism on how the UK can reach its massively ambitious low-carbon generation capacity targets.

"Hydrogen, currently a gas with rather niche industrial applications, must now be acknowledged as an indispensable component of the Net Zero solution."

4. Hydrogen: to the rescue?

4.1 Why hydrogen?

Hydrogen, currently a gas with rather niche industrial applications, must now be acknowledged as an indispensable component of the Net Zero solution. This was recognised by the CCC in its May 2019 Net Zero Report:

> *Moving beyond an 80% target changes hydrogen from being an option to an integral part of the strategy... By 2050, a new low-carbon industry is needed with UK hydrogen production capacity of comparable size to the UK's current fleet of gas-fired power stations.*[41]

National Grid shared this view in FES 2019, forecasting:

> *to achieve net zero emissions, by 2050 natural gas is no longer burnt without the use of CCUS, and so natural gas can no longer be used for residential heating. However, in our Net Zero sensitivity, there is an increasing reliance on hydrogen, which can be burnt without the release of carbon.*[42]

In its Net Zero scenario, National Grid project 47% of gas and electricity use in 2050 will be dedicated to the production of hydrogen (leaving only around 5% of natural gas for heating and gas-fired electricity generation, in both cases with CCUS). That is a complete turnaround from the position today: a move from less than 1TWh of hydrogen being produced now to 324TWh in 2050. Similarly, IRENA projects a 6% hydrogen share of global final energy consumption by 2050 (others project even greater shares).[43]

Hydrogen is non-toxic and abundant in the forms of water and natural gas. When consumed it only releases water vapour, so at the point of consumption it does not share the GHGEs consequences of natural gas. The production of hydrogen is already a very well understood process (albeit the current scale of production is only a fraction of that anticipated in the Net Zero scenarios). It therefore carries a heavy burden of expectation in delivering the solution to a number of Net Zero-induced challenges. These are explored in greater detail below, but include being:

- a flexible energy vector[44] to bridge the gap between rising demand for electricity and increasing levels of intermittent renewable generation;
- a long-term (seasonal) store of energy. As with natural gas, gaseous hydrogen can be stored under great pressure or in very cold liquid form, or by being combined with liquid organic hydrogen carriers (eg, methanol); and

- distributable by repurposing the existing gas network, making it a cost-effective and sustainable replacement for natural gas in residential and commercial heating.

The infrastructure challenge presented by the transition to green hydrogen[45] is significant, but if it can deliver on its early promise then it has the potential to decarbonise substantial sections of the energy system. A 2019 report for the Energy Networks Association projected that a future energy system that uses a balanced combination of low-carbon and renewable gases with low-carbon electricity (as opposed to limiting low-carbon and renewable gas to cases where there is no reasonable alternative energy source, for example, high temperature industrial processes) could be cheaper by as much as £13 billion per year.[46]

4.2 How is hydrogen produced?

Hydrogen is already safely produced in large volumes, but only for quite limited industrial purposes. If hydrogen demand increases significantly along the lines anticipated by National Grid, there would need to be a complete sea change in the hydrogen supply chain. There are two methods of producing hydrogen. The first is by applying

Figure 17: Current UK hydrogen production methods

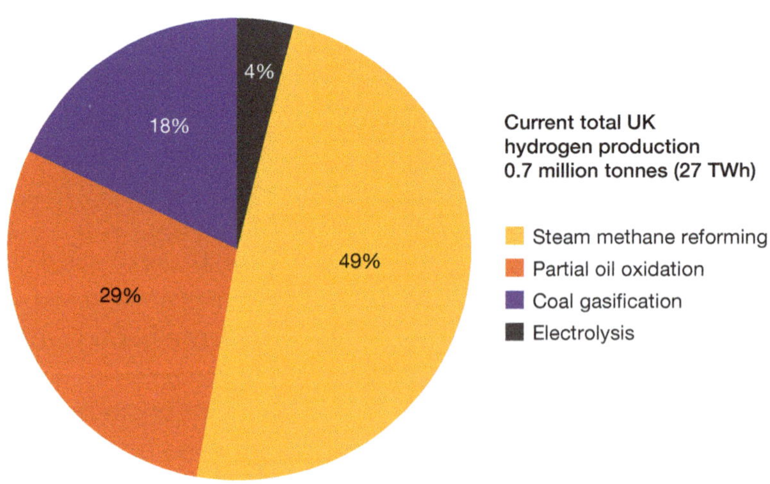

Source: © National Grid's Future Energy Scenarios 2019

an electrical current to water in a process called electrolysis, which produces hydrogen and oxygen. The second, and by far the dominant, is from the combustion of natural gas in steam, in a process called steam methane reforming (SMR).

(a) Steam methane reforming (SMR)

SMR is a multi-step process. Firstly, feedstock, which is generally methane from natural gas, is purified. The purified methane is mixed with steam at high temperatures in the presence of a catalyst. This produces a synthetic fuel, which is a mixture of hydrogen, carbon monoxide and CO_2. The carbon monoxide can be reprocessed with steam to produce more hydrogen and CO_2. Next, the waste CO_2 can be captured with CCS technology.[47] Hydrogen fuel cells (eg, for transport) require higher purity levels, so depending on the proposed application of the hydrogen, additional purification processes can be applied. Finally, the hydrogen can then be transported using new pipelines or by repurposing the existing gas network. Local use or storage solutions can also be developed.

National Grid foresees the large-scale deployment of SMR capability by 2030 (potentially in capacities of up to 1.5GW per plant). There can probably be a reasonably high degree of confidence in this projection as SMR is the dominant process for hydrogen production today. The uncertainty relates to how successfully, and at what cost, CCS technology can be developed and combined with SMR to decarbonise production. The main cost drivers behind expanding SMR production will relate to the costs of natural gas and CCS technology, and the required purity of the hydrogen produced.

(b) Bolting carbon capture storage (CCS) on to steam methane reforming (SMR)

It is worth noting that the addition of CCS will not make SMR-produced hydrogen an inherently carbon-free process. This is because CO_2 capture efficiencies are only expected to reach around 85–95% when the technology is proved viable, meaning the remaining CO_2 still escapes into the atmosphere.[48] That said, current carbon capture pilot projects are at a very early stage and are not yet performing anywhere near this level. As things stand, the development and delivery of CCS and CCUS pilot projects for both power generation and industrial process are some way off-track from that anticipated a decade ago. This suggests that carbon capture technology, and therefore the viability of low-carbon SMR, will not experience a significant scaling up unless capture rates, process efficiencies and long-term storage are all substantially improved. Furthermore, as with the disposal and long-term storage of nuclear waste, it is important that a clear and appropriate liability regime for the stored CO_2 is developed, to ensure parties are incentivised appropriately in what is otherwise a low-margin activity. Hopefully the promise offered by high-volume hydrogen production will provide an additional driver to reach this goal. Carbon capture technology is touched on further in section 5 below.

(c) Electrolysis

Electrolysis is the application of an electrical current to split water into hydrogen and oxygen. There are several different types of electrolysis, which differ depending on which catalyst is used – the main forms being polymer electrolyte membrane electrolysis (PEM) and alkaline electrolysis. At the moment electricity for the process is generally provided by power from the gird (which will include a large proportion of fossil fuel-derived electricity), but the hope is that over time electrolysers will be powered by dedicated renewable energy (producing so called 'green hydrogen').

Although electrolysis has the most potential from a Net Zero perspective, the technology behind it is immature at scale and has some way to develop before the sector can be confident that electrolysis is an efficient and affordable approach to hydrogen production. Smaller electrolysers (<1MW) are used across the world, and they are particularly appropriate for transport fuel where high purity levels are required by fuel cells. Above this capacity, electrolysers are only in pilot phase and have some way to go before their technical and commercial viability is established. As electrolysers are smaller than SMR technology, electrolysis is particularly appropriate for being located in close proximity to the point of use.

Notwithstanding its future promise, the levelised cost of hydrogen (LCOH) for electrolysis is currently almost double that of SMR, mainly due to high electricity prices and slightly poorer efficiency levels. Given the multiples of additional renewable generation required to deliver Net Zero (as explored in chapter IV), there is a significant opportunity for electrolysis to capitalise on that renewable growth, although for that same reason, it is probably unlikely that there will be sufficient renewable capacity to make the economics of electrolysis attractive until after 2030. In the meantime, there are several innovation and pilot projects attempting to demonstrate the commercial and technical viability of electrolysis paired with renewable generation.

From an energy systems management perspective, electrolysers also have the potential to offer demand-side flexibility to National Grid, ramping up or down production rates in response to the varying availability and price of power.

Figure 18 below shows hydrogen production costs from solar and wind versus those of fossil fuels. It contains IRENA's projection that low-

Table 1: Hydrogen production methods in summary[49]

SMR/ATR (with CCUS)	Electrolysis
Potential for significant emissions savings	Zero-carbon production method
Lower overall costs	Can be co-located with local generation
Best efficiencies for large-scale production	Best efficiencies for direct fuelling for hydrogen transport

Source: © National Grid's Future Energy Scenarios 2019.

cost renewables (powering electrolysis) may reach fossil fuel parity (against SMR with natural gas and CCS) within the next five years. A report from the Hydrogen Council in late January 2020 examined a number of existing hydrogen use cases, and concluded that the cost of low-carbon and/or renewable hydrogen production will fall by up to 60% over the decade (and that many of the use cases will become competitive with conventional options by 2030). The predicted cost

Figure 18: Hydrogen production costs from solar and wind versus fossil fuels

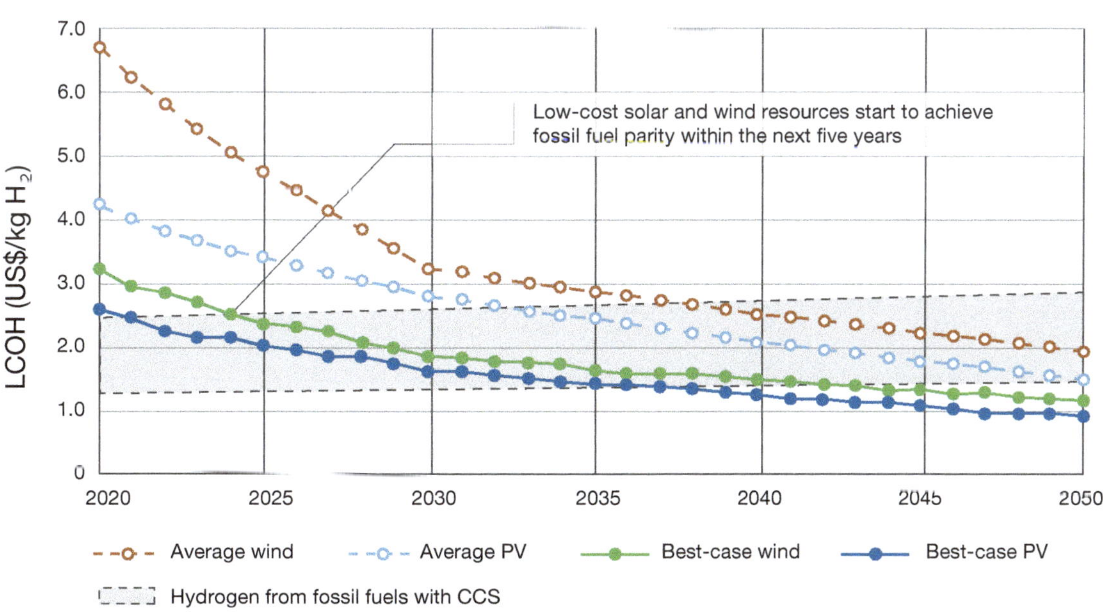

Note: Remaining CO_2 emissions are from fossil fuel hydrogen production with CCS.
Electrolyser costs: 770 USD/kW (2020). 540 USD/kW (2010), 435 USD/kW (2040) and 370 USD/kW (2050).
C0₂ prices: USD 50 per tonne (2030), USD 100 per tonne (2040) and USD 200 per tonne (2050).

Source: © IRENA, Hydrogen: A Renewables Energy Perspective (Sep 2019)

savings are driven by a combination of the falling cost of renewable power; scaling up of electrolyser manufacturing (achieving significant supply chain cost savings); and the development of lower-cost carbon storage facilities.[50]

4.3 Hydrogen and energy storage

There is not yet a consensus about the best approach to hydrogen storage. Once produced, hydrogen can either be stored as a liquid at extremely low temperatures (below -250°C) in dedicated structures (liquefaction), or as a compressed gas in large pressurised storage tanks or underground salt caverns (pressurisation). Pressurisation offers the potential for long-term storage, possibly across seasons and, of the two, is probably more appropriate for the long-term storage of high volumes of hydrogen. Unfortunately, both liquefaction and pressurisation come at the cost of significant energy losses: liquefying hydrogen and keeping it cooled below -250°C consumes huge amounts of electricity. By comparison, liquefied natural gas (LNG) must be stored below -162°C, and the current viability of LNG production relies on very high utilisation rates. Either way, storing hydrogen introduces much lower cycle efficiencies into the process than its immediate consumption in, for example, industrial hubs.

There is also the potential for more innovative storage solutions, for example, by converting hydrogen to energy-dense ammonia for storage or transportation, or even for direct use (without converting back to hydrogen). This means the same volume of transported material can carry a higher density of stored energy. Ammonia (NH_3) is produced relatively simply by combining nitrogen and hydrogen (through the Haber Bosch process), which is also a reasonably simple chemical-engineering process to reverse. This is how it is produced today in the manufacture of fertilisers. As with liquefaction and pressurisation, ammonia synthesis and cracking also consumes a large amount of energy, so, as things stand, there is no silver bullet when it comes to storing hydrogen.

4.4 Applications of clean hydrogen

Once a cost-effective solution to producing hydrogen at scale has been found, it has a number of potential applications to support the delivery of Net Zero:

(a) Industrial

Energy-intensive processes (eg, steel production) use high volumes of primary energy sources. In principle, hydrogen could replace natural gas as the feedstock in these industrial processes to reduce or abolish their associated GHGEs. It could also replace natural gas for the provision of industrial heating.

(b) Transport

The current consensus is that the best low-carbon fuel source for smaller electric vehicles (EVs) is lithium-ion batteries, due to the high costs of hydrogen fuel cell technology and the limited availability of refuelling stations. However, for intensive long-haul vehicles, buses and trains; and in shipping and aviation, there are limited low-carbon options available. Alstom has already made considerable progress with hydrogen trains in Germany (as the electrification of branch lines is cost-prohibitive), which is very promising considering trains account for half of all diesel consumed in the UK. Good progress is also being made in the demonstration of hydrogen fuel cell trucks in Europe and the US.

(c) Power generation

Power generation is perhaps the most interesting application of hydrogen in the medium term (or at least once the costs of producing hydrogen come down). Hydrogen presents both the opportunity to store renewable energy for periods longer than lithium-ion batteries (which may provide an additional driver to the development of renewable power) and to replace natural gas in gas-fired turbines. This is important for maintaining the resilience of the electricity system and providing security of supply in an increasingly intermittent renewables-based generation mix.

"Hydrogen presents both the opportunity to store renewable energy for periods longer than lithium-ion batteries (which may provide an additional driver to the development of renewable power) and to replace natural gas in gas-fired turbines."

(d) Buildings

Around 18% of GHGEs in the UK are associated with heating residential space, generally through the combustion of natural gas in boilers (this rises to around 30% for residential and industrial heating combined). There are a number of pilot studies looking at the extent to which hydrogen can replace or be blended with natural gas, using existing gas networks and boilers. Initial studies indicate that hydrogen can safely be blended to concentrations of up to 20% with natural gas without requiring any change to the existing gas network or customer appliances. This is positive as a 20% blend secures a 6% improvement in GHGEs. Of total natural gas consumed from the gas network, this is a significant saving, and in many respects a quick win for the movement towards Net Zero. Several boiler manufacturers in the UK and Europe have also developed boilers that are designed to burn 100% hydrogen, and it is unlikely to be long until this is a requirement of all new boilers.

Case study: HyDeploy, Keele University

In early 2020, HyDeploy announced that it had successfully injected zero-carbon hydrogen (produced through electrolysis) into the UK's gas grid. This is part of a demonstration project to blend up to 20% (by volume) of hydrogen into Keele University's existing natural gas network. This privately owned network supplies 100 homes and 30 faculty buildings, and the 20% hydrogen blend is the highest in Europe (together with a similar Engie-led project in Northern France). As part of its announcement that the project had become fully operational, HyDeploy drew attention to the fact that heating for domestic and industrial purposes accounts for half of the UK's energy consumption and one third of its carbon emissions, with 83% of homes using gas to keep warm. If a 20% hydrogen blend was rolled out across the country it could save around 6 million tonnes of CO2 emissions every year, the equivalent of taking 2.5 million cars off the road.

Case study: SGN's Aberdeen Vision

SGN's Aberdeen Vision pilot project aims to demonstrate the ability of a region (in this case Aberdeenshire) to convert to clean hydrogen. There are several aspects of the project, including first establishing the commercial viability of injecting 2% hydrogen into the National Transmissions System (NTS) at the St Fergus Gas Terminal and, subsequently, developing a case for constructing a new 100% hydrogen pipeline between St Fergus and Aberdeen. This pipeline would initially supply a hydrogen blend of up to 20%, which could be increased to 100% following a complete network conversion to hydrogen. The project also aims to establish the commercial viability of hydrogen production at St Fergus using SMR paired with acorn CCS technology. Acorn is a project led by Pale Blue Dot Energy that intends to develop a major CCS hub at St Fergus, with associated feeder infrastructure from Peterhead Port and Grangemouth. The CO_2 captured by Acorn would then be transported to and stored in the Central North Sea using existing oil and gas infrastructure.

Case study: HyNet
Similar to Aberdeen Vision , the purpose of the North West HyNet project is to deliver a 'blueprint for the UK hydrogen economy'. It also intends to develop a hydrogen with CCS capability, employing the same industrial cluster approach. A hydrogen production hub (using SMR) is paired with carbon capture technology, with the potential for inter-seasonal hydrogen storage in local salt caverns in the Cheshire basin. Hydrogen can be provided to local customers and businesses (to a 20% blend) or made available as a transport fuelling hub for trains and buses. The CO_2 from the combustion of natural gas in SMR could be transported and stored through repurposed Liverpool oil and gas fields and infrastructure. Over time, the main method of hydrogen production could transition from SMR to renewable energy sources through electrolysis (and the development of a local hydrogen economy may incentivise the further investment in renewable technologies), which would optimise the ability to absorb excess off-peak renewable energy generation and minimise the volumes of CO_2 produced through SMR.

4.5 Hydrogen: two opportunities

The opportunity for hydrogen is twofold. In the first place, the existing process for producing hydrogen is unsustainable without modification. According to figures from the IEA the production of hydrogen, almost all of which is through fossil fuels, consumes 6% of the global supply of natural gas and 2% of the global supply of coal.[51] Natural gas is the dominant energy source for hydrogen production, accounting for around 75% of hydrogen's primary energy source demand. Although it has already been mentioned in this chapter that global production of hydrogen has only quite limited industrial applications, the associated annual CO_2 emissions from the production of hydrogen are (somewhat staggeringly) equivalent to those of the UK and Indonesia combined. Cleaning up hydrogen production for its own sake is no small challenge, let alone exploring its potential as an energy vector of the future.

The second opportunity for hydrogen is in its symbiotic relationship with renewable energy. As mentioned in section 4.2 above, hydrogen for industrial applications is almost entirely driven by SMR (electrolysis only accounts for less than 0.1% of global dedicated hydrogen production because it consumes more energy than can be channelled into the hydrogen it produces). However, with the falling costs of renewable power, particularly from solar and offshore wind, there has been considerable interest in exploring the exploitation of hydrogen through green electrolysis. This could be achieved by co-locating electrolysers with renewable technology in the most favourable solar or wind locations, opening up cost savings from using cheap renewable power when demand is low.

4.6 Hydrogen in 2050

That, then, is the case for hydrogen from a GHGEs perspective. But what will the hydrogen sector look like in 30 years' time when the Net Zero 2050 deadline arrives? There are two competing 2050 projections for hydrogen as a fuel of the future.

(a) Industrialised steam methane reforming (SMR) (blue hydrogen)

This first vision sees large volumes of SMRs having been built within industrial ports, including on existing refinery and chemical production sites along the coast. Hydrogen from these SMRs was initially consumed locally, anchored by baseload consumers from industry and the transport sector. Over time, hydrogen use extended to commercial and residential consumers near the industrial clusters, initially in low blends (<20%) but eventually reaching 100%. These localised hydrogen clusters then spread and connected to each other, forming larger hydrogen zones. By 2050, CCS has been proven at scale and has been successfully paired with SMR plants. Pipelines, being either newly constructed or repurposed from existing offshore oil and gas infrastructure, remove CO_2 from the new SMR plants and transport it to offshore carbon storage facilities (being depleted oil or gas cavities in the North Sea). Monitoring and assurance processes have successfully validated the safe, long-term storage of CO_2 in subsea geological features. The industry has benefited from the investment of sums previously allocated to the decommissioning of offshore facilities.

(b) Renewable-powered electrolysis (green hydrogen)

In response to the high capital cost of CCS, CCS's failure to prove itself technically viable at scale or (unrelatedly) a surplus of available renewable output, this second vision sees the production of hydrogen from electrolysis powered by cheap renewable electricity. The electrolysers are placed in locations most likely to suffer network constraints that would, absent the available electrolysers, lead to the generation being curtailed (ie, paid to not generate). Because the level of utilisation of electrolysers powered solely by constrained renewable power is low (making the associated cost of the electrolysers high), electrolysers have also been placed in locations where it is not

Figure 19: Use and production of hydrogen in the Further Ambition scenario (2050)

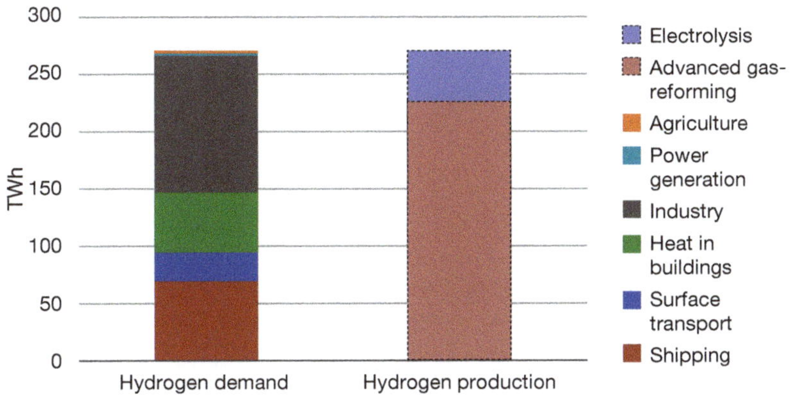

Source: © CCC analysis

Note: The analysis assumes the majority of future hydrogen production in the UK is from advanced methane reformation with CCS (225 TWh), with a limited contribution from electrolysis (44 TWh).

economical to transmit electricity produced by renewable generators over very long distances, including on floating offshore wind clusters in the North Sea and large solar farms in remote desert areas.

In both applications, electrolysis has become viable because it can exploit the low marginal cost of renewable energy. The hydrogen produced is fed into a gas network, stored on site or transported in dedicated trucks or ships. The possibility of shipping hydrogen in liquid form has introduced the opportunity of trading hydrogen in place of LNG, leading to an opening up of energy markets and the introduction of hydrogen as a commodity. While cost savings have primarily been secured through cheaper electricity costs, the wide scale deployment of electrolysers has also driven cost savings through competition and economies of scale in the manufacturing process.

(c) A compromise?

A more realistic outcome may be a compromise between the two visions. Based on the structure of early pilot studies, the most sensible direction appears to be the organic development of demand clusters that form around a growing blue hydrogen production capability (SMR with CCS). Generation, transmission and consumption can be proved at a local level and modified according to what works well. This would be suitable for existing industrial centres where there is both a clear demand for the hydrogen, and a desire to capitalise on early economies of scale and to protect jobs. As these demand clusters grow, they can eventually be joined together through transmission lines. This seems more credible than a wholesale shift to hydrogen of the kind seen in the switch to natural gas in the 1970s. Then, over time, electrolysis may become the dominant production method as it becomes able to capitalise on the cheaper marginal cost of renewable power. This approach sees green hydrogen as the natural end point, with a long transition provided by blue hydrogen.

The CCC projects that in 2050 hydrogen demand is mostly associated with industrial combustion, heavy goods vehicles, heating buildings and power generation. It sees production being dominated by advanced gas reforming, with a minority contribution from electrolysis.

5. Carbon capture technology

5.1 Overview

Several comments about CCS and CCUS have already been made in the natural gas section of chapter V and section 4 above, so they are not repeated here.[52] The premise of CCS is very simple – wherever possible, CO_2 should be captured rather than released to the atmosphere. This is fundamental to the continued use of natural gas in a Net Zero world. At a high level, this requires four separate stages:

- **CO_2 capture:** The CO_2 must be captured from the industrial process associated with its production. This could be by gasification and partial oxidisation of a natural gas fuel before its combustion (pre-combustion capture) or by capturing the CO_2 from the exhaust of natural gas combustion through a chemical absorption process (post-combustion capture).
- **CO_2 transportation:** Captured CO_2 is then compressed and transported through adapted or specially built pipelines, or on ships or road tankers.
- **CO_2 storage:** The best long-term storage option for CO_2 is considered to be injecting it into deep underground rock formations, including depleted or disused oil and gas fields or deep salt cavities/saline formations.
- **CO_2 usage:** There are a variety of uses for the carbon in CO_2 once captured, and it would be reasonable to assume new uses will be found to reflect the increased enthusiasm for a circular and sustainable economy (including in synthetic fuels or in building materials).

The problem with the previous CCS competition in 2015 was that bidders had to provide full CCS delivery chains, from capture to storage. This meant consortia had to define and allocate liability regimes for faults in the delivery chain that may not necessarily be under their control, potentially making the process much more expensive than it had to be. The revival of CCS enthusiasm now has benefited from the disaggregation of the supply chain and the recognition that different funding models and liability regimes may be appropriate for different stages. This has, perhaps, allowed elements of the delivery chain (eg, new capture technologies) to come forward under their own merits, rather than being constrained by the whole delivery chain requirement.

5.2 Carbon capture storage (CCS) and Net Zero

The ability to capture CO2 from industrial and domestic processes is integral to the successful realisation of the Net Zero ambition. This is because energy consumption cannot be exhaustively electrified, and indeed not all electricity generation can be entirely decarbonised. The indispensability of CCS reflects the continuing importance of natural gas in the energy mix, which is why the CCC in its Net Zero report states that "CCS is a necessity not an option". It foresees CCS having a fundamental role in industry, in hydrogen production, in combination with biofuels and in flexible fossil-fired power generation, potentially requiring 75–175 million tonnes of CO2 to be stored annually by 2050. This is echoed in National Grid's FES 2019, where CCUS is regarded as being:

"The ability to capture CO2 from industrial and domestic processes is integral to the successful realisation of the Net Zero ambition."

essential in our Net Zero sensitivity to enable decarbonisation across several sectors, particularly: (i) the widespread production of low-carbon hydrogen in GB; (ii) the use of low-carbon heat for industrial processes; and (iii) the use of negative emissions technology to offset carbon emissions for processes that are very difficult to decarbonise.

The government's Clean Growth Strategy (2017) had already stated an ambition to deploy CCS at scale during the 2030s, subject to costs coming down sufficiently. That cost conditionality has now all but disappeared given CCS's strategic importance in achieving deep decarbonisation; the CCC noting: "Given the lack of progress to date ... progress in deploying CCS in the 2020s is a crucial enabler to putting the UK on track to meeting a net-zero target."

Much like the approach to developing a hydrogen fuel economy set out above, the CCC, National Grid and the wider industry consider regional 'industrial clusters' to be the most appropriate way of encouraging the development of CCS. A number of demonstration sites have been identified and, of these, Zero Carbon Humber, a partnership between Drax, Equinor and National Grid Ventures, and Net Zero Teesside, a partnership between five oil and gas companies, are the most advanced. The ambition of Zero Carbon Humber[53] is to develop a large-scale carbon CCUS network and either CCGT (with carbon capture) or hydrogen production facility in the Humber and Teesside regions by the mid-2020s, to develop what could be the world's first zero-carbon industrial cluster (the concept of developing CCS clusters was promoted heavily in CCC's Net Zero report).

There are several elements to the Humber project, but the core components are

- to install carbon capture technology at Drax's power station (which, when combined with a bioenergy fuel source, would make it the world's first carbon-negative power station);
- to develop a CO_2 transport and storage system across the region (to promote the growth of local industry);
- to develop an approach to securely storing CO_2 deep under the North Sea seabed; and, in so doing,
- to drive the development of a hydrogen fuel economy.

Not all pilot projects fall neatly into this 'cluster' model, particularly where transportation and storage of CO_2 is not a problem. Tata Chemicals Europe is currently developing the largest carbon capture and use project in the UK, which may capture as much as 40,000 tonnes of CO_2 per year when operational. The CO_2 is captured from the flue gasses using advanced amine technology (which absorbs CO_2

"The ability to remove CO_2 that has already been released into the atmosphere is critical to the successful realisation of Net Zero."

from flue gas emissions from the site's CHP plant). As one of the drivers of the project is to reduce the cost base for sodium bicarbonate production (which is the purpose of the site), the captured CO_2 is intended to be used as a raw material for high-grade sodium bicarbonate. As such, the plant does not face the transportation and storage challenges of other CCUS applications, but it is a very good example of both the application of CO_2 capture technology and the recognition that the captured CO_2 has both an environmental value (in reduced emissions) and a commercial value (as a raw material in production and in mitigated carbon prices).

6. Negative emissions

Carbon capture technology is all very well for the continued use of natural gas, but the ability to remove CO_2 that has already been released into the atmosphere is critical to the successful realisation of Net Zero. This is because not all human activity can be entirely decarbonised. Sectors such as farming, which accounts for up to 10% of UK GHGEs, present real challenges for the Net Zero emissions target. The methane produced by ruminants has a warming effect 28 times that of CO_2. Also, certain industrial processes (including chemical manufacturing) cannot easily be decarbonised and carbon capture technologies, even when fitted, are very unlikely to have 100% capture rates. These are referred to as residual emissions.

The delta from zero introduced by these intractable residual emissions means that the Net Zero target involves the delivery not just of zero emissions, but of negative emissions. This means removing CO_2 from the atmosphere that may have been there for many years. There are three approaches to delivering negative emissions:

- reforestation or rewilding;
- capturing CO_2 directly from the air; and
- combining carbon capture with the combustion of biomass.

6.1 Going green: reforestation and rewilding

The easiest and cheapest means of lowering atmospheric concentrations of CO_2 is through reforestation. Encouraging and capitalising on entirely natural processes, the planting of trees and the protection of natural carbon sinks such as peat lands, are all effective means of using photosynthesis to offset GHGEs. Obviously planting the trees is not an end in itself, and protecting those areas over time from threats including forest fires, bush fires and competing land use demands will be critical. Many of the issues surrounding the required changes to land use over the next 30 years are discussed in the CCC's "Land use: Policies for a Net Zero UK", published in late January 2020.

"The easiest and cheapest means of lowering atmospheric concentrations of CO_2 is through reforestation. Encouraging and capitalising on entirely natural processes, the planting of trees and the protection of natural carbon sinks such as peat lands, are all effective means of using photosynthesis to offset GHGEs."

6.2 Direct air capture (DAC)

DAC captures CO_2 directly from the atmosphere through a chemical process. Even more so than CCS and CCUS, it is in very early stages of development but offers the potential for easily scalable deployment (as it is modular technology). As with the production of hydrogen through electrolysis today, DAC is an extremely energy-intensive (and therefore expensive) process. According to an estimate from the National Grid in FES 2019, removing only 25Mt of CO_2 can add 50TWh to electricity demand. Again, much like the comments in relation to the future development of electrolysis above, greater volumes of low-cost renewable power may help drive the growth and commercial viability of DAC technology. Although the potential for DAC is in principle unlimited (CO_2 concentrations in the atmosphere not acting as a constraint), the economics behind its viability will be driven both by the capital cost of the underlying technology and in there being an economically efficient use for the CO_2 captured. Potentially this could be in synthetic fuels, through synthesising the captured CO_2 with green hydrogen.

6.3 Bioenergy carbon capture storage (BECCS)

Biomass already accounts for a considerable amount of renewable energy generation. Although the fuel consumed is organic matter (crops, plants and wood pellets) that has been grown to capture CO_2 from the atmosphere, that CO_2 is then released when the biomass is combusted or processed. This makes it a carbon-neutral process. Combining biomass with CCS offers the potential to permanently remove CO_2 from the atmosphere, making the process carbon negative.

National Grid's Net Zero sensitivity projects the successful delivery of negative carbon emissions through BECCS in the power generation sector and in the production of hydrogen. This scenario outlines that, by 2050, 43TWh of electricity will be produced from BECCS, which will remove 37Mt CO_2 from the atmosphere. The reason for limiting BECCS to power generation is mainly due to the opportunity cost of land use in prioritising biomass feedstock over other agricultural purposes (including the growth of food crops). Similarly, the scalability of the process is limited not only by competing land uses for the feedstock, but also because BECCS requires large power generation plants. Alongside power generation, National Grid also foresees a considerable volume of biogas (produced from the anaerobic digestion of organic matter) being used in industrial CHP plants by 2050.

As referred to above, Drax's Yorkshire coal plant is running a pilot project to demonstrate the viability of BECCS technology in electricity generation. This project aims to capture the CO_2 produced from the combustion of a 100% biomass feedstock, potentially making it the world's first negative emissions power station. The 'capture' stage is piloting the use of an organic solvent (developed by C-Capture) that isolates CO_2 from the flue gasses released after combustion. Although the programme is currently only capturing one tonne of CO_2 per day, if successful it may provide a pathway to scalable BECCS in the 2020s. Obviously the captured CO_2 still has to be either reused or successfully transported and stored, but that is the fundamental challenge of CCS and CCUS technology generally.

7. Advanced nuclear technologies

7.1 Overview

The CCC's Net Zero Report endorsed the role of nuclear in its vision for achieving Net Zero carbon emissions by 2020, noting:

> *Renewable generation could be four times today's levels, requiring a sustained and increased build out between now and 2050, complemented by firm low-carbon power options such as nuclear power and CCS (applied to biomass or gas-fired plant).*

The CCC recognised the role low-carbon power (particularly nuclear) can play in complementing renewable generation, rather than assuming that renewables can rapidly and comprehensively replace all other forms of generation technology.

Similarly, deep in its 2019 Progress Report, the CCC reiterated that:

> *Alongside new renewables, technologies which can offer firm and flexible power, such as nuclear and [carbon capture and storage (CCS)], will be required for a power system in 2050 contributing fully to achieving overall net zero emissions.*

Picking up the thread, National Grid in FES 2019 introduced small modular reactors (SMRs) into its future energy scenarios for the first time. Under its Two Degrees scenario (the publication date of the report meant it could not fully take into account the new Net Zero target), National Grid also predicted the growing role of nuclear in the UK's energy mix from 2030, when most of the UK's existing reactors would start to be replaced, with a projected peak nuclear capacity of 16GW by 2050 (compared to a little over 9GW today). 7GW of this capacity is expected to come from SMRs alone.

Unfortunately, progress in the UK's new build nuclear industry has stalled in recent years, as outlined in chapter V. It was once fêted by policy makers as the best route towards a low-carbon energy future, but the Fukushima disaster in Japan in 2011 led to Germany pulling out of the nuclear industry entirely and to German utilities RWE and Eon

"It was once fêted by policy makers as the best route towards a low-carbon energy future, but the Fukushima disaster in Japan in 2011 led to Germany pulling out of the nuclear industry entirely and to German utilities RWE and Eon withdrawing from the UK's £20 billion new build Horizon project."

withdrawing from the UK's £20 billion new build Horizon project. That was followed by a frustrating few years trying to find an appropriate funding model that worked for new build nuclear plants, eventually leading to the suspension of the NuGen and Horizon projects in 2018 and 2019 respectively. On top of that, extended outages from advanced gas-cooled reactor (AGR) stations (which make up seven of the UK's eight nuclear power stations) have served as a reminder that most of those stations are now in their last few years of useful life.

Nonetheless, the UK government is now keen to support the development of 'small nuclear' to complement the development of the larger Hinkley Point C project (HPC and the large nuclear projects that may follow it are covered in chapter V). Whereas the National Grid referred to SMRs in FES 2019, the breadth of technology now available means the government prefers the term 'advanced nuclear' (or even just 'small nuclear'), which captures the two distinct categories of SMRs and advanced modular reactors (AMRs), as outlined below.

7.2 Small modular rectors (SMRs) (Generation III water-cooled SMRs)
It's probably worth saying that, compared to other forms of generation, there is nothing necessarily small about 'small' SMRs. Their smallness is purely in comparison to 'normal' nuclear stations, and the

modularity aspect is as important a differentiator from the often unique design or site-specific considerations of large nuclear projects (as explained further below). Small nuclear projects can range significantly both in size and cost, for example from microgeneration projects to 600MW reactors, with an associated project cost range of £100 million to £2.5 billion.[54] Although the emergence of operational SMRs in the UK would be new, the technology behind them is actually relatively standard, being a form of conventional light water reactor.

The nascent SMR programme that ground to a halt in 2017 has now been revived by the government's summer 2019 proposal to invest up to £18 million from the Industrial Strategy Challenge Fund in new SMRs. This investment will support a Rolls-Royce-led consortium that is proposing a joint investment of more than £500 million in designing a first-of-a-kind SMR. The government and the consortium anticipate that an initial model could be operating in the early 2030s (the regulatory framework and policy regime will be key in facilitating this, including in appropriately adapting the Generic Design Assessment process for the reactor technology). The number of 'homes powered' (the government's preferred metric for expressing energy capacity) for Rolls Royce's proposal is a quite considerable 750,000 homes per SMR unit.

7.3 Advanced modular reactors (AMRs) (Generation IV AMRs)

The technology behind AMRs is in some way novel, whether that relates to the cooling systems or the fuel types, rather than being scaled down evolutions of existing reactor types, like SMRs. AMRs also have the capability to offer new functionality, for example the production of industrial process heat. The government is also intending to make four grants of up to £10 million each under the advanced modular reactor (AMR) programme.

Although it does not fit neatly into this category, it is worth saying that there remains considerable ongoing interest in nuclear fusion as a potential form of energy generation. In comparison to nuclear fission (the underlying atomic process of existing nuclear plants), nuclear fusion involves two lighter atomic nuclei combining to form a heavier nucleus, while releasing energy – which is the same process through which stars release energy. However, because creating the right temperature and pressure conditions to sustain fusion consumes an awful lot of energy (a plasma must be created in which fusion can occur), there is unlikely to be a significant breakthrough in the immediate future as, with existing projects, more energy is consumed than output created, somewhat defeating the purpose.

7.4 Why advanced nuclear?

The rationale behind small nuclear projects is that they can potentially avoid the three major issues of megaprojects, identified by the Expert Finance Working Group on SMRs as being size, complexity and uniqueness (in terms of explaining the typical budget overruns and delays of large nuclear new build projects).[55] The key is in their modularity, which is really a function of the delivery model rather than the underlying technology (this explains the initial popularity of the SMR acronym).

The principle of advanced nuclear is that smaller units can be produced in factories employing standardised design and modular construction principles. This has the potential to deliver reduced manufacturing lead times and lower capital costs, on the basis that cost savings are ultimately promised through economies of multiples rather than the economies of scale that underpin large nuclear projects (essentially, multiple versions of the same design can be reasonably simply produced in stable conditions).

Accordingly, there is an advantage in using as much proven technology as possible and standardising plant manufacture in a modular factory environment. Relocating construction activity from sites to factories helps minimise both construction risk (including weather-related delays) and the need to retain a skilled workforce on site for prolonged build periods. That said, the modules do need to be easily transportable by road and it will be important that their design is complete before construction begins. On the basis that it will be (thereby avoiding expensive mid-construction design changes), standardising production in this way will help de-risk the manufacturing and installation process, which should ultimately lead to a lower cost of capital and, therefore, cheaper overall delivery model.

Advanced nuclear also has a number of additional benefits beyond modular construction and a stable factory build environment. Some of these reflect the general trend in the electricity industry for a move from baseload to more flexible, distributed generation. Examples include:

- being able to deliver both baseload and flexible power (not a characteristic of existing nuclear);
- the ability to use existing nuclear sites (perhaps alongside those sites being decommissioned);
- the possibility of being co-located with other technologies (eg, electrolysers for hydrogen production);
- faster build times; and
- the ability to deploy advanced nuclear projects in remote locations.

"Electricity is not an easy commodity: it is indispensable to the modern economy; not conducive to long-term storage; in need of continuous real-time balancing of supply and demand; challenging to transport; supported by complex and capital-intensive infrastructure; often loaded with policy agendas; and subject to constant price volatility."

VIII. The UK's electricity network: electrons in balance

1. Overview

Daily activity is increasingly digital and conducted online and, as we know, this is all underpinned by electricity.[56] It is difficult to characterise precisely the complexity of the electricity system. Electricity is not an easy commodity: it is indispensable to the modern economy (as illustrated by the outcry following any blackout); not conducive to long term storage; in need of continuous real-time balancing of supply and demand; challenging to transport; supported by complex and capital-intensive infrastructure; often loaded with policy agendas; and subject to constant price volatility. Accordingly, reliable capacity and flexibility have become increasingly prized characteristics. Electricity is also at the heart of the now somewhat unfashionable 'energy trilemma', which is an expression of three interdependent characteristics of energy – that it should be:

- secure (have sufficient capacity to meet peak demand);
- affordable (with around one in ten UK households thought to be in fuel poverty);[57] and
- sustainable (meaning it is provided through low-carbon fuels).

Almost above anything else, the electricity system has become bound-up with the drive to decarbonise our economy. While a lot has been done to ensure electricity remains affordable (notwithstanding the significant proportion of an energy bill made up of network costs and low-carbon support mechanisms), the real policy interest in electricity over the last decade has been on decarbonisation. This means designing energy policy so that it becomes a tool to combat climate change. In fact, unlike other fronts in the battle against climate change (eg, decarbonised heating, improving energy efficiency and the electrification of transport), the decarbonisation of power generation is comparatively well advanced.

2. The electricity system: what it is and how it works

This electricity network is made up from the high voltage transmission system (owned and operated by three transmission owners as geographical monopolies) and the lower voltage distribution system (owned and operated by 14 distribution network operators, which are owned by six different organisations). Currently, there is 108GW of generation capacity in the UK, split as 71% transmission connected, 24% distribution connected and 5% microgeneration. National Grid electricity system operator (National Grid ESO) manages the overall system and ensures the real-time balance of electricity supply and demand. This description from National Grid ESO's website is a useful introduction to the network:

> *It can be helpful to think of GB's electricity system in terms of our road network. National Grid, a legally separate company to the ESO, owns the motorways, or the transmission network. The ESO uses these motorways to run high voltage electricity through the system until it gets to the B roads, which are privately owned local distribution networks. From there smaller operators – Distribution Network Operators, or DNOs – reduce the voltage and take electricity to peoples' doors. Connected to these networks are privately owned power stations, which are separate from National Grid. They generate and feed electricity into the network.*[58]

Beyond the physical infrastructure of cables, towers and transformers, the UK electricity market is essentially a description of the interaction between the following market participants:

2.1 Generators

Generators own power-generating assets (which range in terms of complexity from large-scale nuclear plants to small anaerobic digesters) and export the electricity they produce onto either the transmission or distribution network. Generators hold a generation licence under the Electricity Act 1989 which entitles them to generate electricity for the purpose of supplying premises.

2.2 Transmission operators (TOs)

The 400 and 275 kilovolt (kV) high-voltage transmission system (which in Scotland also includes the 132kV system) is owned, operated and maintained by transmission operators (TOs). There are currently three licenced TOs, each of whom operate the high voltage system within their respective onshore transmission areas. These are National Grid Electricity Transmission plc (NGET) for England and Wales, Scottish Power Transmission Ltd for southern Scotland and Scottish Hydro Electric Transmission plc for northern Scotland and the Scottish islands.

2.3 Transmission system operator (TSO)

While the transmission network is owned and maintained by the TOs, the electricity system as a whole is managed by a single ESO. Following its formal separation from NGET in 2019, that role is performed by National Grid ESO. National Grid ESO is licensed under the Electricity Act 1989 and is required to "develop, maintain, and operate economic and efficient networks and to facilitate competition in the supply of electricity in Great Britain". National Grid ESO has no responsibility for the electricity infrastructure itself, but has a crucial role in ensuring that demand and supply are continuously balanced.

2.4 Distribution network operators (DNOs)

The distribution networks carry electricity from the high voltage transmission network across lower voltage networks to industrial, commercial and residential customers. There are 14 licensed distribution DNOs in the UK and each is responsible for a regional distribution services area. As well as the DNOs, there are also a number of smaller networks owned and operated by independent network operators (IDNOs) within the areas covered by the DNOs. As with the TOs, to prevent the possibility of price abuse arising from their natural monopoly position, the DNO's pricing regime is heavily regulated (under Ofgem's RIIO price control regime).

2.5 Traders and aggregators

Traders optimise electricity assets by buying and selling power directly (or bilaterally). There are four ways of trading wholesale electricity:

- Internal transfers within vertically integrated companies (that is, companies that have both a retail business and a generation business), such as EDF Energy, Centrica/British Gas and SSE.
- Bilateral contracts, either through power purchase agreements (PPAs), tolling agreements or standard 'over the counter' trades using the Grid Trade Master Agreement (GTMA). This is how the majority of electricity in the UK is traded.
- Over electronic power exchanges (eg, APX).
- Through the BM (see section 3.1 of this chapter), which could be characterised as a form of residual pool.

2.6 Suppliers

Suppliers buy electricity from generators (or are part of a vertically integrated organisation that has its own generation business) and supply that power to industrial, commercial and residential customers. Suppliers (unless they fall under a relevant exemption) hold a supply licence which allows them to supply electricity to premises. An electricity supply licence can be for supply to domestic and non-domestic premises, or non-domestic premises only. Profit margins for UK suppliers are incredibly tight at the moment, not helped by the high levels of subsidies and network costs that flow through to the customer's final bill (see below) and the introduction of the default tariff cap in 2019. This compounds the existing challenges of a volatile wholesale market and the difficulties in managing fixed costs – particularly with the growing rate of customer switching.

2.7 Customers (industrial, commercial and residential)

Customers buy electricity from the supplier and pay for both the cost of power and the associated cost of delivering that energy. Like a £5 bottle of wine, the cost of wholesale power (or wine) actually makes up a surprisingly small proportion of each customer's energy bill (only around 33%).[59]

Figure 20: Breakdown of an electricity bill

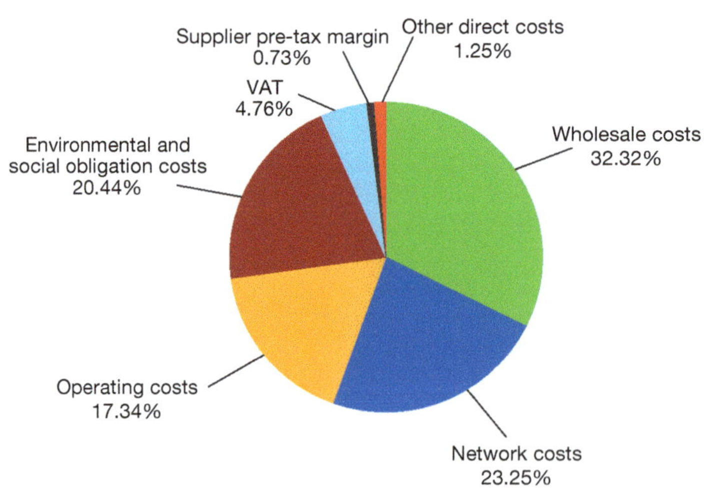

Source: Adapted from Ofgem, www.ofgem.gov.uk/data-portal/breakdown-electricity-bill

2.8 Ofgem and the Department for Business, Energy and Industrial Strategy (BEIS)

BEIS is the government department responsible for the development and implementation of energy policy. Ofgem is the energy industry regulator and develops the framework to deliver that government policy. Its roles include:

- consulting with industry on proposed changes;
- monitoring the market and compliance by market participants with their licences;
- investigating alleged breaches of licences; and
- liaising with other regulators.

Ofgem is particularly concerned with protecting vulnerable consumers (particularly around fuel poverty) and promoting competition in the gas and electricity markets.

There is an important distinction between the physical and commercial delivery of electricity. Physical delivery is the act of moving electricity from generators over transmission and distribution networks to customers. Commercial delivery is a description of the transfer of economic and legal interest in that electricity as it moves around the system. A supplier (eg, one of the 'Big Six') will contract with a generator and with a customer to buy and then sell power, but it will never actually 'hold' that electricity itself. This underscores the important and growing role of data in driving and maintaining an efficient market.

3. Balancing the electricity system: the balancing mechanism (BM) and ancillary services

3.1 The balancing mechanism (BM)

The first line of defence in maintaining a balance between system supply and demand is the accurate forecasting of that demand. This provides a reference point for generators and suppliers to forecast their own required levels of activity. To the extent demand is not accurately forecast, the BM allows National Grid ESO to correct the imbalance in electricity supply and demand at the delivery point (meaning at the time electricity is actually exported to the grid by a generator and imported by a supplier). In relation to each half-hour 'settlement period', National Grid ESO has to match the level of electricity being supplied by generators with the level of electricity being consumed by offtakers. The balance of electricity has to be continuously managed because it is not possible to store electricity at high volumes and because either generation or demand (when delivered or consumed) may differ from that forecast. In relation to forecast activity, registered generators and suppliers must publish

Photo 6. Electricity pylons

Source: © Brian Matthews, published with permission

details of their intended level of generation or offtake for each settlement period. They do this through the use of physical notifications (PNs). Due to the high likelihood of a discrepancy between forecast electricity supply and demand during a certain settlement period, generators and offtakers are required to submit 'bids' and 'offers' to either decrease or increase generation (for generators) or demand (for offtakers).

Although the BM is very important for maintaining the overall system balance of supply and demand, most electricity trading actually happens in the wholesale market (well ahead of the BM timescales). Depending on the scale of a generator or the demand profile of an offtaker, they will generally contract with each other for every half-hour delivery period, often several seasons or years in advance. Recently, there has been a tendency towards shorter-term trading, which means trading in time periods closer to the relevant delivery period. This can include 'day ahead' and 'on the day' trading. In part, this trend towards trading closer to the delivery point is driven by the growing proportion of wind and solar generation, whose intermittent generating profile makes it hard to guarantee delivery at long points in the future (unlike, for example, nuclear which has a very predictable generating profile around its scheduled outages).

Another option for a renewables project is to use aggregators. Aggregators build a mixed profile of generation assets and, with the increased capacity and diversity of technology in that trading portfolio, are able to trade the capacity on behalf of the individual projects in a more flexible manner than would otherwise be available to the individual project owners trading on their own behalf. With the closure of the renewable subsidy schemes discussed in chapter IV, revenue from the wholesale and balancing markets has become even more important to small renewable projects. Accordingly, greater numbers of aggregators are emerging who can help provide a route to market for these smaller projects, who do not otherwise have the capability or accreditation to access these revenue streams themselves.

Electricity trading can continue up to one hour before each relevant half-hour settlement period. At this point 'gate closure' occurs, which indicates that trading for that settlement period has stopped and the BM begins. National Grid ESO is notified of all trading activity by BM participants leading up to gate closure through PNs, so that the trading position for each generator is known. Following gate closure, to the extent there is an imbalance in any of the trading activity, National Grid ESO can accept bids and/or offers to turn up or down generation and/or supply over the level notified at gate closure. For example, if there will be an oversupply for a particular settlement period, National Grid ESO could accept a bid from a generator to turn down its supply and a bid from a supplier to increase its demand (and conversely, an offer from a generator to increase generation or from a supplier to reduce demand). In so doing, it will obviously have regard to any constraints on the system that would affect the ability of a particular supply option to meet the relevant demand (eg, arising from local network reinforcement works). The process of instructing bids or offers is referred to as the instruction of bid-offer acceptances (BOAs) to individual BM participants. BM participants must then act on the instruction to ensure that their BM Units adjust their output/demand profile accordingly. Any failure to deliver in accordance with the forecast supply or demand position exposes the relevant BM participant to an imbalance payment, which broadly reflects the cost to National Grid ESO of having to 'correct' the imbalance.

3.2 Wind and the balancing mechanism (BM)

Somewhat counterintuitively, wind now has quite an influential role in the BM. This is surprising because most BM and ancillary services activity focuses on either conventional flexibility (mainly small gas plants or diesel) or new flexible technologies, including fast-discharging grid-scale batteries. While wind does not have the same 'dispatchable' capabilities of synchronous turbines or batteries, its growing prominence on the system means it plays a crucial role in helping National Grid ESO manage network constraints, supply and demand imbalance and increasingly (as coal plants close) the loss of inertia. When wind is instructed in the BM it is generally for accepted bids (to turn down generation). Generally, wind cannot 'offer up' because it is already financially incentivised by the ROC regime (for ROC-supported projects) to maximise its generation, as RO payments are received on a MW/h output basis. It is possible for wind to generate at less than 100% availability so that it can then ramp up to meet demand, but the cost of doing this is the lost ROC (or applicable subsidy support) and power price.

Onshore wind has a particularly close relationship with system constraints for geographical reasons. Generally, high wind output in Scotland needs to be moved to high demand areas in south England, for example, through the Western Link high voltage direct current (HVDC) subsea cable which commissioned in November 2019. When there are system issues in the high voltage transmission system, National Grid ESO often has to pay constraint payments to onshore wind generators to turn down production. Because they have to factor the cost of lost subsidy revenue, wind bids in the BM tend to be negative, as the RO proportion of their revenue is so significant (negative pricing means a payment is made to generators to decrease their output). Constraint payments for wind hit record highs in 2019, exceeding £8.5 million in August alone. Issuing constraint instructions 'wastes' the otherwise zero-carbon generation these turbines can produce – which is why co-located storage and the introduction of new technologies such as hydrogen production and storage through electrolysis have become so popular.

3.3 Ancillary services

(a) Overview

As the BM operates so close to the point of delivery, the reality is that it is only really appropriate for fine tuning overall system balance. More substantial balancing activity actually takes place through the procurement of 'ancillary services' by National Grid ESO. Ancillary services refer to the provision of other types of services by generators on top of their primary activity of generating electricity. The procurement of ancillary services is becoming increasingly important for two reasons. First, as the subsidy mechanisms available to renewable projects has been withdrawn, project developers have been increasingly motivated to exploit other revenue streams. Traditionally, ancillary services contracts have provided a lucrative (and low-effort) income source to a project on top of its primary generating activity. However, the emergence of more renewable projects and a weaker wholesale price has led to far more competition for these ancillary contracts. The price awarded in successive tender rounds has therefore fallen.

"Onshore wind has a particularly close relationship with system constraints for geographical reasons. Generally, high wind output in Scotland needs to be moved to high demand areas in south England, for example, through the Western Link high voltage direct current (HVDC) subsea cable which commissioned in November 2019."

The second reason for the importance of ancillary services is that the overall generation profile has changed considerably over the last decade (as set out in chapter III). From a system management perspective, this means the availability of certain tools that were perhaps taken for granted (eg, inertia provided by traditional 'spinning turbine' generators) now have to be actively procured. It also means that the overall generation profile is far less predictable than it used to be. The intermittency of wind and solar means National Grid ESO has to take a more active role in procuring ancillary services to balance out the intermittency. Some of the issues associated with the changing generation mix were seen on 9 August 2019 when there were localised blackouts following lightning strikes to transmission infrastructure that caused a drop in system frequency and the associated tripping of two separate power generators (the Hornsea offshore wind farm and Little Barford CCGT).

(b) Frequency response

The National Electricity Transmission System operates at a frequency of 50Hz, with National Grid ESO being under an obligation to maintain frequency within the statutory limit of +/-1% of that figure (ie, within a stable range of 49.5–50.5Hz). System frequency is determined by the balance between generation and demand. If demand exceeds generation, frequency falls. If generation exceeds demand, frequency rises. Frequency is like a long line of mini-dominoes in an electricity cable connected by a central wire; if that wire becomes too lax (frequency dropping) the line of dominoes falls over. Frequency continuously oscillates and National Grid ESO procures a range of frequency response services to help maintain it in a stable range. If frequency moves outside this range (as it did for example during the 9 August blackout referred to above), electrical systems automatically trip to maintain overall system integrity. If a sufficient volume of generation capacity trips, frequency falls to a level where low frequency demand disconnection is triggered and load automatically trips in groups of low frequency relays, causing localised blackouts. This demand shedding, although drastic, helps stabilise system frequency. It is complemented by battery storage and fast-response generation, including pumped storage and gas turbines, promptly coming online. This avoids a disastrous whole-grid shutdown and the need for a 'black start' of the network.

Generators that operate in 'frequency response mode' are able to quickly respond to frequency deviations by automatically increasing or decreasing output, with the response typically being provided within seconds. Response is either provided on a continuous basis where second-by-second frequency variations are monitored

"Battery storage developers often draw attention to the benefits of immediate frequency response for the first few minutes of a grid-scale incident, to maintain system stability until larger generators are able to respond at greater capacity and for longer durations."

(referred to as 'dynamic frequency response') or where a response is only triggered at a defined frequency deviation threshold, which may for example happen when a generator has tripped (referred to as 'static frequency response'). National Grid ESO's need for frequency response services is highest when system inertia is low, as frequency deviations move faster when inertia is low, as explained in the inertia section below. 'Enhanced frequency response' refers to the one-off 2016 tender for 200MW of capacity that was contracted to deliver sub-second response services. This form of fast-responding service is particularly suitable to grid-scale batteries, and accordingly it is battery projects that have competed particularly strongly in frequency response tenders. Battery storage developers often draw attention to the benefits of immediate frequency response for the first few minutes of a grid-scale incident, to maintain system stability until larger generators are able to respond at greater capacity and for longer durations.

(c) Inertia
Inertia is the physical description of an object's tendency to continue in its current state. This means, absent an opposing force, a stationary object will remain stationary and a moving object will continue at its current speed and trajectory. Inertia has traditionally played a particularly important role in maintaining frequency on the grid, as it is able to slow down the rate of change of frequency (RoCoF). With the mini-dominoes point above – this would be like filling the cable with treacle – it slows down how quickly the dominoes fall over or are pulled tight.

Inertia is a natural characteristic of the electricity system because of the mechanical motion of spinning turbines. All UK spinning turbines are electrically linked (synchronised) to the frequency of the grid. The kinetic energy in spinning turbines provides a natural and free supply of inertia to the grid, meaning they soften frequency deviations from the target 50Hz. The level of inertia on the system determines how quickly frequency will change when an imbalance arises between generation and demand. A common analogy is that of car shock absorbers, which smooth out the impact of jolting potholes on the road.

With the increasing penetration of non-firm generation that has no rotating mass (primarily wind and solar), the proportion of generation made up of spinning turbines is falling. This means National Grid ESO is losing its inherent supply of inertia. As system inertia decreases with the changing energy mix, the RoCoF has a tendency to increase. Rather than attempting to emulate synchronous generation and procure supplies of inertia to replace turbine generation (which it regards as an expensive option), National Grid ESO's strategy has instead been to limit the largest infeed loss (for example by instructing the largest generator to limit output). This is to minimise a significant RoCoF if that generator were unexpectedly to fail (this issue will become even more relevant when Hinkley Point C commissions and becomes the largest generator on the system). That said, there may now be a slight change in this approach as, in early February 2020, the UK became the first country to award contracts for 'inertia only' services.

There has also been some progress with the development of 'synthetic inertia', the idea being that solar and storage are able to react so quickly that they can simulate the effect of rotating mass inertia (and perhaps even do so more accurately). To offer this at a significant scale, solar projects would have to change their operating profile. Rather than running so as to maximise generation at all times (as incentivised by the FiT regime), they could hold back some generation capacity to be ready to increase generation if frequency drops (by producing at lower levels). An alternative is to integrate onsite storage and provide reserve capacity through the volume of generation that is held back in storage (ready for immediate dispatch if frequency drops). The project owner would have to be compensated for this 'loss of generation' for the relevant volume of headroom, but that is no different in theory from compensating spinning reserve; or it could be expressly compensated as an 'inertial response emulation' service. That approach would simulate the effect of inertia through tracking system frequency and controlling power output accordingly.

(d) Reactive power

'Active power' (measured in watts/kilowatts/megawatts) is the form of electricity that satisfies domestic and commercial energy demand. 'Reactive power' is what 'pushes' the active power around the grid (although it is not itself a force) and is important because of its effect on system voltage. The UK transmission system has to stay within 5% of 400kV (or 275kV), and the ability of a unit to absorb or generate reactive power helps deliver voltage stability (generating reactive power increases voltage on the system). Reactive power is generated in the same way as active power but it is fed into the system differently. It also only has a short-lived, localised effect. Traditionally, there have been a high number of intensive users of electricity (eg, large manufacturers) and this has meant generators have been required to generate reactive power to maintain system voltage. As the electricity system has become increasingly decentralised and demand from large industrial consumers has fallen, it is now more common for generators to be required to absorb reactive power. This is because the falling load on the system increases voltage, so generators are required to absorb reactive power to compensate. It is possible for wind and solar farms to deliver reactive power although, as things stand, there is little financial incentive for them to do so.

(e) Reserve power

Reserve power is needed to compensate for the imbalances that arise from forecasting errors and unexpected losses on the system (see comments above, section 3.1). There are various forms of contracted reserve power, and they are generally concerned with compensating for an unexpected drop-off of the largest generating unit on the system:

- **Frequency response:** An unexpected drop of generation will cause frequency to fall, so reserve power is a form of ancillary service that can enhance or decrease system frequency.
- **Spinning/fast reserve:** This service provides a rapid and reliable delivery of active power through an increase in generation output or a reduction in demand, and is procured through monthly tenders. Service providers are required to ensure active power delivery can start within two minutes of an instruction and the response must be capable of delivering a minimum of 25MW (before March 2019 it was 50MW). Generators can, for example, run at partial load (eg, 50% of output capacity), so they are in a position to quickly ramp up or ramp down in response to demand changes. Hydro and pumped storage also have the ability to respond to generation demands in a very short space of time.

"Traditionally, there have been a high number of intensive users of electricity (eg, large manufacturers) and this has meant generators have been required to generate reactive power to maintain system voltage. As the electricity system has become increasingly decentralised and demand from large industrial consumers has fallen, it is now more common for generators to be required to absorb reactive power."

- **Short-term operating reserve (STOR):** This service provides additional active power from an increase in generation or a reduction in demand, and is procured in relation to a number of 'STOR seasons'. Service providers have a target response time of around 20 minutes and should be able to sustain a response for at least two hours. This service was traditionally provided by diesel generators but it is now also possible to procure a similar service from battery and DSR participants. STOR is National Grid ESO's largest balancing services market, with over 2GW of capacity retained for short-term demand balancing requirements (providing sufficient capacity to meet unforeseen outages or rapid-demand changes).
- **Demand turn up:** When there is unexpected surplus power on the grid, industrial and intensive energy users can be instructed to increase their demand or prioritise a grid-provided supply over their own embedded generation. This is most typically required during periods of high renewable output and low national demand, which is generally overnight and during weekend summer afternoons. It is a flexible service focused on the near term and is not regarded as an enduring solution for 'negative reserve' (compare with fast reserve and STOR for positive reserve). The requirements are less formal than the other services. As the system increasingly moves away from large, transmission-connected thermal generation, National Grid ESO anticipates DSR will have an increasingly important function in system balancing (and in avoiding the need for costly network reinforcement works).

(f) Blackstart

Blackstart services enable the restoration of the electricity network when the transmission system or a large part of it shuts down during a blackout. The provider of the service is required to have its own onsite auxiliary generation which can start without power from the grid (to create an 'island' independent of the transmission system). This small power island can then power up other local assets and eventually the relevant part of the system. The risk of blackstart is not new or necessarily increasing, but the availability of large baseload generators that have traditionally provided the service (eg, coal stations supported by onsite diesel generators) is falling – so National Grid ESO is looking at new flexible ways of providing the service. This could, for example, include a combined CCGT/large battery response service.

(g) Future of ancillary services

The various services described above reflect a patchwork development of responses that National Grid ESO has required to help it balance the system. However, the electricity system was designed with large baseload spinning turbines and energy-intensive industrial users in mind. The future electricity system is increasingly distributed, intermittent and disaggregated. The consequence of that, unfortunately, is that the existing portfolio of ancillary services is now in many respects overlapping, inconsistent, opaque and insufficiently anticipatory of the decreasing dominance of synchronous generation. As the generating mix has started to change, there is a clear need to harmonise the procurement of these essential services – something National Grid ESO is currently taking a very close look at.

"Achieving Net Zero will require fundamental changes to personal behaviour: in the way we eat, travel, consume energy and use land. None of the other objectives will materialise through the unsolicited top-down imposition of didactic policy."

IX: Looking forward

If confidence in the deliverability of Net Zero by 2050 hangs in the balance, 2020 may well prove to be the fulcrum. 2020 has been touted by the government as being the "year of climate action", particularly in the lead-up to Conference of the Parties (COP) 26 in Glasgow. It is also an obvious point at which we are able to look back and recognise the scale of the challenge that has built up behind us, and to look forward and consider practically, with an open mind, what it will take over the next 30 years to bring our net GHGEs down to zero. This is the question the UK has been quick to compel itself to answer, but the challenge is a global one and the answer must be found collectively if the laudable ambition of the Paris Agreement is to be realised.

Looking back, then, we see behind us a mixed picture globally. On the one hand, global emissions have continued to rise steadily, hitting a new high in 2018 and putting us on track for a 3.2°C average temperature rise by the end of the century (against a target of 2°C or 1.5°C). Hitting the 2°C target will require at least a 2.7% drop in emissions each year to 2030. Yet on the other hand, global investment in renewable capacity is rising significantly, with the previous decade seeing more than treble the amount invested in renewable energy capacity than the one before it. Equally, renewable technologies have seen unprecedented cost savings, with most falling into, or even beyond, the global-weighted average LCOE range for fossil fuels.

The UK has seen a significant fall in its own GHGEs since 1990 (although this must be balanced by the observation that many of its most carbon-intensive activities have been offshored). It has partly achieved this through focusing on energy efficiency and sustained growth in renewable power, which now accounts for around 33% of electricity generation (with coal having fallen to just 3%). But that trajectory has been interrupted by the closure of most of its renewable subsidy schemes to new projects, with levels of onshore renewable investment consequently having fallen catastrophically in 2018 and 2019. To reclaim the renewable growth narrative, the UK must be quick to define and tirelessly promote a coherent policy framework that can deliver a credible route to the Net Zero destination. That is the task facing the UK, and expectations of the imminent and much-delayed energy white paper are high.

The scale of the challenge for the UK is remarkable. It is worth repeating some of the observations from chapter IV:

- 263 GW of low-carbon power may be required by 2050, up from 108 GW of installed generating capacity now (around half of which is fossil-fuelled).
- The majority of existing forms of generation will need to be replaced or repowered by 2050.
- The renewable share will need to increase by at least a factor of four.
- There will be a substantial reliance on technologies that are still quite some way from operating at scale.

The electricity system too (and its attendant regulatory regime) will have to adapt from being a baseload, transmission-dominated network to one that increasingly relies on high levels of intermittent renewable and embedded generation. The smart time shifting of demand in response to the availability and price of electricity will become a key characteristic of the consumption of energy. As mentioned elsewhere in this report, all of this will be driven by the need to decarbonise electricity and to electrify more of our energy consumption.

How will this be achieved? The imperative now is to look forward and to plan effectively for the next 30 years. A policy framework must be generated that has, at a minimum, the following key objectives:

- the delivery of large volumes of renewable and low-carbon investment in a sustained and cost-effective way, with the aim of facilitating approximately 10GW of new capacity each year;
- the endorsement of an investable funding model for new build nuclear (RAB or otherwise), that recognises and learns from criticisms and failings of previous projects;

- the promotion of viable technologies and funding models for each stage of the CCUS pathway, in recognition that the capital spend and risk profile of each part is different;
- the delivery of a hydrogen model, underwritten by an appropriate combination of SMR (with CCS) and electrolysis, that has the capability to incrementally displace our reliance on natural gas;
- a coordinated transport policy that recognises the challenges of EV and hydrogen infrastructure but also the opportunities decarbonised transport can present; and
- perhaps most importantly, the conversion of hearts and minds in a manner akin to the sudden move against plastics.

Achieving Net Zero will require fundamental changes to personal behaviour: in the way we eat, travel, consume energy and use land. None of the other objectives will materialise through the unsolicited top-down imposition of didactic policy.

The widespread public, commercial and organisational adoption of more ambitious localised Net Zero targets has been extraordinarily encouraging. But there is a danger presented by the overreaching of initial good intentions over practical achievability. If we see well-publicised quick wins but a clearly articulated pathway to a common goal is not delivered, there is a danger of the momentum being lost.

At this point, the critics will start to make their voices heard, giving voice to the doubts that run like stress fractures through the whole enterprise:

- "Net Zero is too expensive."
- "The practical implications are too difficult."
- "It is imperialistic."
- "It makes any first mover fundamentally uncompetitive, the emissions gap [discussed in chapter II] is growing too quickly."
- "The reductions required have become too extreme."
- "A watered-down target is more sensible."

When making the amendment from 80% to 100% net GHGE reductions, the government indicated their intention to review the position after five years. What will the mood be at that time?

This is quite some challenge for the early 2020s. But it is also a remarkable opportunity for those active in the industry and those with a concern about the environment we live in. It is shaping up to be a fascinating start to the new decade.

Notes

1 "As far as the future is concerned, it is not a question of predicting it, but of making it possible." French writer and aviator de Saint-Exupéry is quoted in the IPCC's Special Report, "Global Warming of 1.5°C" (available at www.ipcc.ch/sr15/) to underline the need for urgent, transformative action in the energy industry and other greenhouse gas-emitting sectors.
2 IPCC Special Report, "Global Warming of 1.5°C", 2018. Available at: www.ipcc.ch/sr15.
3 According to the IEA, coal (as a fuel/source) accounts for 38% of global electricity production; natural gas 23%; hydro 16%; nuclear 10%; solar PV 1.7%; wind 4.4%; oil 3.3%; biofuels 1.9%; and geothermal 0.3%. See IEA Statistics Report, "Renewables Information 2019". Available at: www.iea.org/reports/renewables-information-2019.
4 UN Environment Programme, "Emissions Gap Report 2019". Available at: www.unenvironment.org/resources/emissions-gap-report-2019.
5 IPCC Special Reports: "Climate Change and Land", 2019, available at www.ipcc.ch/srccl/; and "Special Report on the Ocean and Cryosphere in a Changing Climate", 2019, available at www.ipcc.ch/srocc/.
6 *BP Statistical Review of World Energy* (68th ed), BP, 2019. Available at: www.bp.com/content/dam/bp/business-sites/en/global/corporate/pdfs/energy-economics/statistical-review/bp-stats-review-2019-full-report.pdf.
7 UN Environment Programme, "Emissions Gap Report 2019", *supra*.
8 IEA press release, November 2019, "World Energy Outlook 2019 Highlights Deep Disparities in the Global Energy System". Available at: www.iea.org/news/world-energy-outlook-2019-highlights-deep-disparities-in-the-global-energy-system.
9 The UN's Emissions Gap report (*ibid*) notes that existing pledges are therefore incompatible with the Paris Agreement goals, and that countries need to increase their contributions (referred to as Nationally Determined Contributions (NDCs) under the Paris Agreement) threefold to achieve the "well below 2°C" goal and more than fivefold to achieve the 1.5°C goal.
10 US Energy Information Administration, *International Energy Outlook 2019*, September 2019. Available at: www.eia.gov/outlooks/ieo/pdf/ieo2019.pdf.
11 UN Environment Programme, Frankfurt School-UNEP and BloombergNEF, *Global Trends in Renewable Energy Investment 2019*. Available at: https://wedocs.unep.org/bitstream/handle/20.500.11822/29752/GTR2019.pdf.
12 Solar Photovoltaic (PV) is the generation of electricity by converting sunlight (solar radiation) into direct current (DC) electricity using semiconductors. When the sun hits the semiconductor within the PV cell, electrons are freed within the cell and form an electric current. Solar PV technology is generally employed on panels (hence solar panels). Solar PV systems therefore concern the generation of electricity, whereas thermal solar systems are used for the direct heating of water or air. In particularly hot climates, thermal solar can nonetheless be used to generate electricity using energy from the sun to heat a fluid to a high temperature, by concentrating the sun's rays on one point to achieve very high temperatures; this is called concentrated solar power (CSP).
13 UN Environment Programme *et al*, *Global Trends in Renewable Energy Investment 2019*, *supra*.
14 *Ibid.*
15 *Ibid.*
16 IEA, World Energy Outlook special report, "Offshore Wind Outlook 2019", November 2019. Available at: www.iea.org/reports/offshore-wind-outlook-2019.
17 *BP Statistical Review of World Energy*, *supra*.
18 UN Environment Programme *et al*, *Global Trends in Renewable Energy Investment 2019*, *supra*.
19 IEA, Market Report Series, "Renewables 2019", October 2019. Available from: https://webstore.iea.org/market-report-series-renewables-2019.
20 IEA, World Energy Outlook special report, "Offshore Wind Outlook 2019", *supra*.
21 DNV GL, "Energy Transition Outlook 2019". Available at: https://eto.dnvgl.com/2019/#Energy-Transition-Outlook-2019.
22 US Energy Information Administration, *International Energy Outlook 2019*, *supra*.
23 International Renewable Energy Agency (IRENA), *Renewable Power Generation Costs in 2018*. Available at: www.irena.org/-/media/Files/IRENA/Agency/Publication/2019/May/IRENA_Renewable-Power-Generations-Costs-in-2018.pdf.
24 UN Environment Programme *et al*, *Global Trends in Renewable Energy Investment 2019*, *supra*.
25 The intermittency of renewable technology is a much discussed topic. One interesting development has emerged from the growth of the offshore wind sector: as turbines have become larger and further offshore, they can access stronger and more regular wind flows, and accordingly achieve lower variability of output (ie, lower intermittency). This has prompted the IEA to categorise them as "the only variable baseload power generation technology", due to their capacity factors of 40–50%. By comparison, solar has an annual average capacity factor of less than 20%. See IEA, World Energy Outlook special report, "Offshore Wind Outlook 2019", *supra*.
26 Source: BEIS, "UK Energy in Brief 2019", available at: https://assets.publishing.service.gov.uk/government/uploads/system/uploads/attachment_data/file/857027/UK_Energy_in_Brief_2019.pdf. Figures in the report are taken from the 2019 edition of the "Digest of UK Energy Statistics", available at: www.gov.uk/government/organisations/department-for-business-energy-and-industrial-strategy/about/statistics.
27 Many of the figures used in this chapter are based on data produced by the Digest of UK Energy Statistics (DUKES) (*supra*). There is often a considerable delay in the availability of data for

generation produced in the preceding year, so it has been updated where possible with quarterly updates at the point of publication. Beyond that, the purpose of this chapter is to indicate the trends in the UK, so any ageing of the precise numbers is not a major concern.
28 Baseload refers to the constant, minimum level of demand on an electrical grid over a period of time, on top of which are daily demand fluctuations (referred to as peak load). Baseload generators are those associated with providing this minimum or base level amount of power, and are typically plants that do not change their power output quickly, such as large coal and nuclear plants.
29 There is a nuance here, explored later in the chapter: the legislative requirement is to procure that total greenhouse gas emissions (GHGEs) in 2050 are reduced by 100% of the equivalent levels in 1990. However, the CCC acknowledges that emissions cannot be reduced entirely, so other methods of removing CO_2 from the atmosphere have to be found (eg, through tree planting), to offset the difference.
30 The Renewable Energy Directive (RED I) committed EU member states to source 20% of the EU's total energy requirement (and for the UK, 15% of its total energy requirement) from renewable sources by 2020. The overall EU target has now been expanded by RED II to 32% by 2030. RED I is available at: https://ec.europa.eu/energy/en/topics/renewable-energy/renewable-energy-directive/overview. RED II is available at: https://ec.europa.eu/jrc/en/jec/renewable-energy-recast-2030-red-ii.
31 BEIS, "2018 UK Greenhouse Gas Emissions, Provisional Figures". Available at: https://assets.publishing.service.gov.uk/government/uploads/system/uploads/attachment_data/file/790626/2018-provisional-emissions-statistics-report.pdf.
32 CCC, "Net Zero – The UK's contribution to stopping global warming" (the "Net Zero report"), 2019. Available at: www.theccc.org.uk/publication/net-zero-the-uks-contribution-to-stopping-global-warming/.
33 See IEA, "The Role of Gas in Today's Energy Transitions", July 2019. Available at: www.iea.org/reports/the-role-of-gas-in-todays-energy-transitions.
34 Specifically, only where operators can establish that the relevant biomass conversion project will lead to a net reduction in atmospheric carbon levels within 10 years. The climate policy thinktank Sandbag (in its December 2019 report "Playing with Fire") has also campaigned against the increased use of biomass by EU states, particularly because the carbon emitted when the biomass is burned will take many years to be reabsorbed by biomass growth. The report is available at: https://ember-climate.org/wp-content/uploads/2019/12/2019-SB-Biomass-report-1.7b_DIGI.pdf. They recommend investment in wind and solar instead of biomass, in supporting the move away of fossil fuel use. That said, as explained in chapter VIII the CCC sees an important role for biomass when paired with carbon capture technology (bioenergy carbon capture storage (BECCS)), as a means of securing 'negative emissions'.
35 See www.ge.com/renewableenergy/wind-energy/offshore-wind/haliade-x-offshore-turbine.
36 A recent report by BloombergNEF found that battery prices have fallen 87% in real terms, from above £844 per kilowatt hour (kWh) in 2010 to £120/kWh in 2019. The report projects that by 2023, average battery prices will be close to £77/kWh. See BloombergNEF's Battery Price Survey 2019, available at: https://about.bnef.com/blog/battery-pack-prices-fall-as-market-ramps-up-with-market-average-at-156-kwh-in-2019/.
37 RenewableUK and Scottish Renewables, *Floating Wind: The UK Industry Ambition*, October 2019. Available from: www.renewableuk.com/store/ViewProduct.aspx?id=15079206.
38 European Wind Energy Association, *Deep water: The next step for offshore wind energy*, 2013. Available at: www.ewea.org/fileadmin/files/library/publications/reports/Deep_Water.pdf.
39 See American Geosciences Institute, "What are the advantages and disadvantages of offshore wind farms?" Available at www.americangeosciences.org/critical-issues/faq/what-are-advantages-and-disadvantages-offshore-wind-farms.
40 Dr M Hannon, E Topham, J Dixon, Dr D McMillan and Dr M Collu, *Offshore Wind, Ready to Float? Global and UK Trends in the Floating Offshore Wind Market*, University of Strathclyde, DNV GL, Energy Systems CDT and Supergen Wind, 2019. Available at: https://strathprints.strath.ac.uk/69501/.
41 CCC, "Net Zero" report, 2019, *supra*.
42 National Grid, "Future Energy Scenarios", July 2019 (FES 19). Available at: http://fes.nationalgrid.com/media/1409/fes-2019.pdf.
43 IRENA, *Global energy transformation: A roadmap to 2050*, 2019. Available at: www.irena.org/publications/2019/Apr/Global-energy-transformation-A-roadmap-to-2050-2019 Edition.
44 An energy vector is a carrier of energy rather than a source of it. When used in relation to hydrogen, it refers to hydrogen's ability to carry energy from either electricity or a fossil fuel energy source, until that store of energy is subsequently consumed (eg, in a hydrogen fuel cell or in combustion).
45 Green hydrogen refers to hydrogen produced through electrolysis using renewable energy sources. By comparison, grey hydrogen is produced through natural gas or coal-powered steam methane reforming (SMR), and blue hydrogen is SMR combined with carbon capture and storage (CCS) technology.
46 Navigant Consulting (for the Energy Networks Association), *Pathways to Net-Zero: Decarbonising the Gas Networks in Great Britain*, October 2019. Available at: www.energynetworks.org/assets/files/gas/Navigant%20Pathways%20to%20Net-Zero.pdf.
47 Reference is made in this chapter to both CCS and CCUS. The first traditionally refers to the concept of capturing CO_2 from a process that produces it (such as the combustion of natural gas in

a combined cycle gas turbine (CCGT) plant) and transporting and storing that CO2 underground. The addition of 'U' in CCUS refers to the 'use' of CO2, the idea being that CO2 can be captured from an industrial process and reused rather than simply released into the atmosphere – for example in fizzy drinks or synthetic fuels. It is worth noting that this will avoid CO2 release at the point of original use (eg, combustion in the CCGT) but not when the CO2 is reused (eg, when the fizzy drink is consumed or the synthetic fuel burned).
48 IRENA, Hydrogen: A Renewable Energy Perspective, September 2019. Available at: www.irena.org/publications/2019/Sep/Hydrogen-A-renewable-energy-perspective.
49 Based on current evidence.
50 Hydrogen Council, *Path to hydrogen competitiveness: A cost perspective*, January 2020. Available at: https://hydrogencouncil.com/wp-content/uploads/2020/01/Path-to-Hydrogen-Competitiveness_Full-Study-1.pdf.
51 IEA, "The Future of Hydrogen: Seizing today's opportunities", June 2019. Available at: www.iea.org/reports/the-future-of-hydrogen.
52 The issue with storage is a policy one as much as a technical one – if CO2 is, for example, injected into depleted offshore subsea oil and gas fields, who retains the long-term liability associated with its continued retention underground? How would such a regime be adequately monitored and verified?
53 The Zero Carbon Humber Partnership, "Capture for Growth: A roadmap for the world's first zero carbon industrial cluster", November 2019. Available at: www.drax.com/energy-policy/capture-for-growth-zero-carbon-humber-report/#chapter-1.
54 Expert Finance Working Group on Small Reactors, "Market framework for financing small nuclear", BEIS, August 2018. Available at: www.gov.uk/government/publications/market-framework-for-financing-small-nuclear.
55 *Ibid.*
56 A 2016 article in *The Independent* by environment editor Tom Bawdon indicated that data centres consumed about 3% of the global electricity supply (which is more than the UK's total electricity consumption) and accounted for about 2% of total GHGEs. That carbon footprint is about the same as the airline industry. Article available at: www.independent.co.uk/environment/global-warming-data-centres-to-consume-three-times-as-much-energy-in-next-decade-experts-warn-a6830086.html.
57 Fuel poverty is defined as circumstances where more than 10% of household disposable income is devoted to energy bills.
58 See www.nationalgrideso.com/about-us/what-eso-and-what-does-it-do.
59 See www.ofgem.gov.uk/data-portal/breakdown-electricity-bill.

About the author

Hugo Lidbetter
Partner, Fieldfisher
Hugo.Lidbetter@fieldfisher.com

Hugo Lidbetter is a partner in Energy and Natural Resources at Fieldfisher, specialising in policy and legal issues relating to low-carbon energy and the zero-carbon agenda.

An energy and infrastructure lawyer with 10 years' experience, he advises international and domestic clients on project development work in the energy sector, including conventional (coal and gas) and low-carbon (nuclear and renewables) power projects.

Hugo has particular expertise in construction law in the energy industry, including advising on industry-standard forms as well as bespoke forms of EPC and O&M contracts, and associated ancillary commercial agreements.

He brings a blended private practice and in-house background, having recently spent five years in EDF Energy's Generation legal team. His role at EDF involved managing an experienced team of lawyers in delivering support to EDF's fleet of nuclear, coal- and gas-fired stations, as well as its gas storage sites and renewables investments. He was also company secretary of the thermal business division.

Having worked in-house for several years, Hugo has a broad understanding of the key areas of law applicable to, and regulatory requirements of, energy companies and how external counsel can add the best value. As a company secretary, he also appreciates the operational and strategic pressures facing a board of directors.

With two young children, Hugo's spare time is spent climbing trees, playing football and dodging arrows. When time allows, he enjoys running, rugby and wistfully dreaming of the days when he can travel again.

About Globe Law and Business

Globe Law and Business was established in 2005, and from the very beginning we set out to create law books which are sufficiently high level to be of real use to the experienced professional, yet still accessible and easy to navigate. Most of our authors are drawn from Magic Circle and other top commercial firms, both in the UK and internationally. Our titles are carefully produced, with the utmost attention paid to editorial, design and production processes. We hope this results in high-quality books which are easy to read, and a pleasure to own. All our new books are also available as ebooks, which are compatible with most desktop, laptop and tablet devices.

We have recently expanded our portfolio to include a new range of journals and Special Reports, available both digitally and in hard copy format, and produced to the same high standards as our books. We'd very much like to hear from you with your thoughts and ideas for improving what we offer. Please do feel free to email me at sian@globelawandbusiness.com with your views.

Sian O'Neill
Managing director
Globe Law and Business
www.globelawandbusiness.com